Praise for *Girls' Club*

Sally and I have committed ourselves to lifelong friendship, and she has given me the richness of her life. We've shared so many memories and are indeed kindred spirits. Together we have prayed, visited each other in the hospital, traveled to Italy and England, and shared many cups of our favorite tea. We will always share memories, nostalgia, and so much fun as we both are committed to our friendship. I pray that through this book you will be encouraged to seek out or embrace friendships where you give and receive.

PHYLLIS STANLEY
Sally's, Sarah's, and Joy's mentor and dear friend

Forty years ago, God gave Sally and me a friendship that was to be for life. It was a gift that became a lifeline as we ministered behind the Iron Curtain and has since seen us through many seasons of life. Sally's family also became a gift to me, and my special friendship with Sarah and Joy has delighted my heart. God has enriched my life through these three Clarkson girls.

GWEN TODD
Committed friend of Sally's for forty years

Friends are not easy to find. Moving to a new city as an adult brought deep loneliness and isolation. Amid a family medical crisis, I forced myself to do what I had seen Sally do so often—initiate and invite new women into my life. Years later, I now count those women among my own girls' club as we travel through life together, taking intentional time to grow our friendships. *Girls' Club* offers both hope and inspiration for finding and tending deep, meaningful friendships. I cannot wait to read this with "the girls."

JENNIE NELSON
Mother of three and friend of Sally's

In a world of constant, instant, worldwide connection, women still find themselves feeling lonely. We are told this is "just the way it is"—that all women are competitive and lean toward comparison and judgment, and that friendship is a thing of the past. But is that true? The Clarkson women are here to issue a challenge and a vision: mothers and daughters, sisters and friends, coworkers and neighbors gathering together around a common purpose to share hearts and dreams and life. As a member of Sally's team, I am a grateful recipient of their encouraging example, have experienced it myself, and am so glad they've written down their hearts to inspire a new generation of women who might just want to initiate their own girls' clubs all over the world.

MISTY KRASAWSKI
Sally's friend of many years

Sally, Sarah, and Joy capture the essence of cultivating friendship. In a culture where women are busy and distracted, it can seem difficult to have meaningful, lasting connection. But the Clarkson women light a candle in the darkness with *Girls' Club* and inspire us through sharing their wisdom and stories of intentional moments curated over years. Sally has faithfully lived out this message in our friendship through the many ways she nurtures, mentors, and inspires me to cultivate friendships that will last a lifetime.

GRETCHEN ROBERTS, MD
Pediatrician and mother of five

In a world of social media, it's easy to forget how to cultivate real friendships. You can invite anyone to "like" you . . . but do you really know them? This book will challenge you to grow godly, loving, authentic friendships that will enrich your life.

SANDRA MADDOX
Ministry leader and Sally's close friend

Friendships with other strong women are what have kept me on track during so many hard, questioning times in my life. It's so important to spend time investing in those relationships, because these friends are the ones who will be there to give you a pep talk, let you cry, or tell you when you're off track!

REBECCA MOON
Business owner and Joy's lifelong friend

Making close, lasting friendships with other women is incredibly important, but the way to those friendships can sometimes seem a bit mysterious! Which is why I'm so excited about *Girls' Club*, an affirming, encouraging look at the beauties (and the practicalities) of developing and maintaining intentional friendships that empower and strengthen us as women. And, as someone who's been blessed with Joy's friendship, I can heartily attest to her expertise on the subject.

ELENA TRUEBA
Writer and graduate student at Harvard Divinity School; Joy's college roommate

Friendships are so important in walking a strong spiritual life. The first time I heard Sally speak, I knew she was a kindred spirit. Now I look back on the years of our faithful friendship, and I thank God for a friend who encouraged me and shared much along the way. *Girls' Club* will encourage you to make committed friendships a priority.

LYNN CUSTER
Sally's friend and companion in life and ministry

To anyone who has ever felt the loneliness of the "connected" digital age, *Girls' Club* is a veritable roadmap to building lasting, faithful friendships—a must-read.

KATHERINE HARLEY
Dear friend and social media specialist to Sarah

One sunny morning in Oxford, fresh off a plane and deposited by a bus onto a cobbled street, my daughter and I (in desperate search of strong tea!) unintentionally wheeled our suitcases smack dab into a meeting of the *Girls' Club*. Right away, I ascertained that this was a sacred circle, a convivial assembly of mutual affection and affirmation. And with this gem of a book, the Clarkson women are pulling up a chair and inviting you, through stories of their own friendships, to widen the lens of possibility for the relationships in your life as they share their hearts, with warmth and wit, about how to combat the isolation of this modern, restless world and embrace God's design to forge and fortify the bonds of friendship with other women. Maybe you think you don't have the time or emotional energy to cultivate deep and lasting friendships? Don't waste another moment in loneliness and fear of rejection! Glean from *Girls' Club* how to initiate the spark that kindles a steady blaze of brave, purposeful, enriching kinship with others who can challenge you to meet fear with courage, dispel spite with kindness and grace, and heal woundedness with generosity of soul.

STEPHANIE WILBUR
Old friend and kindred spirit of Sarah's

Few friendships have shaped my own life the way Sally Clarkson's has. Spending countless hours in her home throughout the last decade, exploring cities together, feasting, talking over tea, and working alongside one another are memories I cherish, but they are also moments that have awakened my heart to the intimate friendship of God, His love for me, and His desire for all of us to have rich relationships that nourish and transform our souls. Now Sally and her incredible daughters have pulled back the curtain on how they have forged friendships in their family and in all the places they inhabit. We are all invited to join the Girls' Club as the Clarksons welcome us not only into fresh hope and practical help for building beautiful ties with other women but with God as well.

KRISTEN KILL
Mother of five and author of *Finding Selah*

Girls' Club

Cultivating Lasting Friendship in a Lonely World

Sarah, Sally & Joy Clarkson

TYNDALE
MOMENTUM®

The nonfiction imprint of
Tyndale House Publishers, Inc.

Visit Tyndale online at www.tyndale.com.

Visit Tyndale Momentum online at www.tyndalemomentum.com.

TYNDALE, *Tyndale Momentum*, and Tyndale's quill logo are registered trademarks of Tyndale House Publishers, Inc. The Tyndale Momentum logo is a trademark of Tyndale House Publishers, Inc. Tyndale Momentum is the nonfiction imprint of Tyndale House Publishers, Inc., Carol Stream, Illinois.

Girls' Club: Cultivating Lasting Friendship in a Lonely World

Designed by Eva M. Winters

Edited by Stephanie Rische

Unless otherwise indicated, all Scripture quotations are taken from the *Holy Bible*, New Living Translation, copyright © 1996, 2004, 2015 by Tyndale House Foundation. Used by permission of Tyndale House Publishers, Inc., Carol Stream, Illinois 60188. All rights reserved.

Scripture quotations marked NASB are taken from the New American Standard Bible,® copyright © 1960, 1962, 1963, 1968, 1971, 1972, 1973, 1975, 1977, 1995 by The Lockman Foundation. Used by permission.

Scripture quotations marked ESV are taken from *The Holy Bible*, English Standard Version® (ESV®), copyright © 2001 by Crossway, a publishing ministry of Good News Publishers. Used by permission. All rights reserved.

For information about special discounts for bulk purchases, please contact Tyndale House Publishers at csresponse@tyndale.com, or call 1-800-323-9400.

ISBN 978-1-4964-3214-8 HC
ISBN 978-1-4964-3215-5 SC

Printed in the United States of America

25	24	23	22	21	20	19
7	6	5	4	3	2	1

We dedicate this book to each other.

Contents

Introduction

SALLY ✌ I love women. I love the way they love each other and encourage one another. I love the way they civilize their homes and nurture their families. I love their generous hearts for reaching out to others, for making things beautiful. I love watching them exert influence as writers, inspire others through teaching, use their gifts of healing in the medical profession, counsel with wisdom, lay spiritual foundations as mothers, pass on a legacy of traditions, and accomplish countless other feats of goodness.

I admire women's ability to work diligently and endlessly through all kinds of demanding circumstances. Yet women flourish most when they cultivate deep friendships, work side by side towards great purposes, and comfort and care for one another in the challenging moments of our stories. Such women in my life have taught me profoundly important values and have inspired me to serve more humbly and to persevere and endure, faithfully trusting God through dark times. They have also shown me the glory of celebrating big and small events in my life. Women seem to know how to be thoughtful, kind, and creative in the most mundane details of life.

I love being a woman. Women must have been kissed by God, because they have been created with immeasurable potential to accomplish beautiful feats and to inspire others through all the centuries of history. Women are natural civilizers and bring dignity and grace to their environments and worlds.

My deep respect for the capacity and scope women hold has come over a lifetime of developing friendships with women who have called me to my best self. Friendships with women of great hearts, engaged minds, and devoted, vibrant souls give me energy to fuel my life and to respond in kind to their initiation. When we connect ourselves, walking arm in arm, we find models of inspiration in the stories of others that spur us on to live into our own potential.

We all long for deep connection because God created us to love deeply, to share our innermost selves intimately, and to enjoy life to its fullest with kindred spirits. The design for sweet and close friendship is imprinted on our hearts by the fingers of God.

Fellowship, deep connection, and kinship among women has been a rich reality throughout all cultures and centuries. No matter the difficult circumstances that may have surrounded them, women came to appreciate their God-given heritage and to understand the legacy of love, wisdom, and skill they could live into by seeing it played out before them organically, day in and day out, with a community of women who lived close by.

It is not so easy for us to see that pattern anymore. It seems to me that women in the twenty-first century have either forgotten the intrinsic potential they have as human beings and as women sharing in friendship and community, or they are just too distracted, overwhelmed, and busy to access the glory and beauty of their femininity and how it blooms more fully in the context of loving relationships. And of course, we are the most connected generation technologically and the most isolated from our neighbors. In our day, everything about womanhood and gender has been called into question, so that many are afraid or reticent to embrace the delight and joy contained in female friendships, the strength that is gathered in communities of women living harmoniously in support of one another, and the encouragement of affirmation that comes from mutual commitment.

I am so grateful that excellent women have been sprinkled along my life path. These women have invested deeply in my own emotional and spiritual health. I never could have written books, had a national and local ministry, finished the course as an intentional mother in my home, and stayed faithful to my marriage without the help, support, comfort, and strength I received from other women. Differing in age, personality, educational background, and life experience, they have each added a grace to the treasure chest of wisdom stowed inside my heart. Each has helped me to flourish when otherwise I would have floundered.

As I began to grasp and appreciate this kind of intentional mentoring, love, and encouragement in my own life, it became a poignant focus of relationship that I wanted to pass on to my daughters. Understanding that influence is best cultivated through love and friendship, I sought to deepen my sympathy for what was going on in their hearts, to understand their personalities, to affirm their intrinsic worth to me and to God and to others, and to encourage them on a daily basis.

One of my overriding goals, though, was to mentor them in their faith. I wanted to pass on a vision for life that would help them cultivate clarity for their place in God's Kingdom work through the living out of their own personal stories. Believing in God's love for them in all circumstances and His presence every minute of their lives was the foundation for passing on deep convictions and faith.

A part of mentoring them in their faith was to challenge them intellectually, as well. Knowing we are called to worship God with our minds, I determined to expose them to great thoughts through the best of writers, to the work of musicians and artists, to the stories of history and the consequences of decisions made in the swirl of real life. Longing to stretch them to their full capacity, I devoted thought, commitment, and time to my relationship with them and to the focus and purpose of the hours we spent together.

Out of this desire came a commitment to regularly gather over many years and to grow in our friendship and to become kindred spirits with one another. Over a period of time, we dubbed our threesome "Girls' Club." We don't remember how the name evolved, but somehow we began to refer to our times together this way, and the phrase stuck. When we would plan an evening together, we would say, "We have Girls' Club tomorrow night," and we all knew what that meant.

At first, we met on Tuesday evenings when Joy, my younger daughter, was a wee girl of seven or eight and Sarah, my older daughter, was about eighteen. (My husband, Clay, would take the boys, Joel and Nathan, who were teenagers at the time, away from the house. Usually they went out to dinner and then to a computer store, a bookstore, or someplace they could talk, and they had a sort of "boys' club.") Though the age difference among the three of us was great, I just focused on developing a close kinship among us. And now Sarah and Joy have become best friends because of all the time spent together and the years invested in cultivating the same preferences.

We always started the evenings by eating something we loved, such as quiche, tea sandwiches, or French food, and most often, some chocolate. We would watch a girl movie, make an evening picnic, give each other facials, paint our toenails, light candles, put on music, and spend fun time together. As time went on, we read books together, went to art museums, looked at magazines, and went for long walks. The girls traveled and worked alongside me as I spoke at events and conferences. This meant that our mutual appetites for life were shaped together through seasons, in ministry, in home, in travel, and in work. After a while, I noticed the talking time became more precious and took longer because we were becoming one another's best friends and wanted to talk about everything. We decided our club would be a weekly commitment, giving us a reprieve from the busyness of life and creating a sense of centering for all the other demands that swirled through our days.

Loneliness was one of the motivations for the Girls' Club through the years. We moved seventeen times—six times internationally. We all found ourselves lonely for people who were familiar and knew us deeply. We looked for friends who were at our stage of life and loved the same values, habits, and delights, and yet we knew that deep friendship comes slowly. I wanted the girls to feel, even during their lonely seasons, that they did indeed have deep friendship. And so Girls' Club helped us create community with each other so that the loneliness wouldn't be felt so acutely. We had each other, and we made it a priority to spend time together.

Having weekly Girls' Club meetings began a tradition that tied hidden strings of love and influence from one heart to another. Our friendship also formed bonds of spiritual connection and faith as we developed our spiritual convictions and as we shared ideas or philosophies or inspirational stories as a part of our shared communion with one another. I think our closeness was forged because of our commitment to keep this engagement every week, with few exceptions. I never saw my daughters just as "the ones I wanted to influence" but always saw them as equals with their own personalities, their own contributions to add, their own thoughts and dreams to be cherished by us all. They were indeed my closest friends.

Eventually, we took planned Girls' Club trips together—to Asheville, Santa Fe, Seattle, Prince Edward Island (Anne of Green Gables land), London, Oxford, Cambridge, Vienna, Poland, and more. Often it was the three of us, sometimes just two. Of course, I feel very privileged to have been able to take them to these places with me, but it was a part of my own personal story and the places I was called to work and live. These were places where I spoke at conferences and met with groups of women. Then we stayed and played for a couple of days afterwards.

During our travels, we always played our favorite music in the car. Joy became our DJ, as she had a knack for choosing different artists and a wide variety of music. In these new cities, often alone in a hotel room, we watched movies, frequented museums, toured on trains, experienced missions, read books out loud, listened to audiobooks, and cultivated friendships with other people, young and old, together.

I know you might be saying, "I wish I had such a life!" Maybe you feel like you could never develop such a friend. But I am convinced that all of us not only have capacity for deep friendships, we *need* them to be able to live emotionally healthy lives. Each of us has a different life story, but all of us have the ability to beautify the days we are given by choosing to grow strong in love, initiation, and imagination with other women and to celebrate life with them.

Through this time of intentional friendship, we have shaped one another and built lifelong bonds that have enhanced and enriched our lives. I honestly did not know how fulfilling it would be to not only mother such excellent women but to see them become my best friends, who now mentor me in so many ways. Both girls are in graduate school now, and I literally take notes about books they are reading, ideas they are exploring, and recipes they have tried.

Over the years, as our pursuits took us all over the world and the girls moved into their own arenas, they each started their own informal Girls' Club groups with the friends present in their lives. Each of us began to see, once again, the strength and encouragement that comes from intentionally creating a community of kindred spirits with women who live near us.

This book is our story as well as a gathering of convictions that each of us holds about the importance of cultivating female friendships that not only provide emotional affirmation and acceptance but also inspire, educate, train, and stretch us to live into our God-given potential. As we seek to invest our lives for God's glory—and satisfy our longing for meaningful and intimate companionship— we are held firm by the friendships we have invested in over time. Cultivating such friendships may take years of making memories, sharing seasons, and initiating, but these friendships become the backbone that holds our lives together.

Some of the stories in this book are repeated several times. That is because some experiences over the years serve as anchors to our times together, giving us stability and a firm foundation. These memories established patterns and gave us ideas about how to create the same beauty or bonding times for future relationships. I hope you will give us grace as you see some of these memories repeated. We may remember these incidents in our own unique ways, but more than that, I hope our stories will serve as an encouragement about what is really worth focusing on, what has stayed in each of our minds as we have established common bonds.

Besides this book, we have also written a companion guide called *Girls' Club Experience* that we hope you will use in your own friendships or community of women or within your own home—as mothers, daughters, sisters, and friends. The companion book is a sort of friendship guide to provide pathways of understanding into each other's stories and lives. You can go through the whole book with a friend or a group, or you can pick and choose from any chapter to find the topic and activity that seems like the best fit for you right now. It is our hope that many Girls' Clubs will start all over the world and that great friendships will be forged through the application of the principles found in this book and the guidebook.

I am a different person because of the faithfulness, encouragement, and inspiration I have received from my friends and my daughters. It is our hope that this book will encourage you to take the initiative to seek out women with whom to share and shape life. We pray that some of our ideas might spawn other meaningful groups and friendships. We hope you will discover anew the gift of intimate companionship with women who support each other, helping each other live up to the amazing potential God created in each of us.

SARAH ✌ I think I must have been about two and a half years old when a babysitter of mine had the audacity to suggest that I was too little to be my mother's friend. At least, that's how I heard it. In one of those childhood memories that is oddly vivid, I clearly recall sitting at the kitchen table of our Viennese house, listening as my mom chatted with this woman. I remember gathering my courage to say something sympathetic to my mom— I think it was about the inconvenience of a recent thunderstorm that fried the electricity—only to be met by the slightly rolled eyes of the babysitter and her patient declaration that "I was too little to understand."

I can still remember the fierce, hot indignation that instantly suffused my small heart at those presumptuous words. I remember even better the retort that came to my mind, the truth that glowed in me: *Mama and I are friends. Of course I understand.* Even better, I recall my mom's gentle hand on my shoulder as I glared at the babysitter and she said, "Oh, Sarah's my pal. I couldn't have done without her. She didn't get scared once, and we got all the candles lit together."

It may seem a small instance—a tiny offense, a little act of kindness by my mom, the quirky memory of a slightly fierce two-year-old. But my mom's words in that moment were a gift, the opening in my memory of the friendship we would share through-out my childhood, one that continues in ever fuller expression to this day now that I am a woman and a mother myself. In that response, my mom invited me into the circle of a delightful cama-raderie, a sharing of life, a recognition of little me as someone who was needed and capable—an invitation that has shaped my con-cept of womanhood and friendship and energized our relationship through all the years that followed.

The joy I felt in that moment of knowing myself my mom's pal, of sharing life in all its storms, lasts even into the present as I now welcome my own daughter into the fellowship I have already known with my mom and my sister. In my heart glowed the radiant knowledge that we were "the girls." We did things together. We were strong. We were friends. We kindled lights in the darkness.

That was the moment, for me, that the Girls' Club began, though of course, it wasn't complete until my sister joined the ranks of the family, eleven years and five days after I did (not that I was counting the days until I finally had a sister). But most of what we three write about in this book could be traced back to the themes I remember in that childhood moment of outrage and triumph. Much of what we hope you will discover in these pages and find yourself equipped to create could be encapsulated by my two-year-old realization of "us girls" as comrades, as strong, as loyal, as capable of all sorts of friendship and creativity amid the storms of life. What we have to write here is simply the story of what we have gained and discovered over decades of the Girls' Club friendships we have cultivated with each other and with other wonderful women, and the way those relationships have enriched our lives.

Friendship seems scarcer somehow these days. Whether it's the busyness of modern life or the way the internet keeps us in a virtual world, away from each other, or just the deep sense of loneliness that is part of the human condition but is somehow heightened in our mobile, anonymous age, real companionship of soul and life is something we have to fight to recover. But oh, what a gift it is, and what we have to write here is the story of that gift, of women who choose and nourish, cultivate and defend the gift of friendship. What we have to relate is the grace and strength that women find in companionship, in sharing the woes of housework and study and work and the wonders of Scripture, the depths of loneliness and the heights of laughter.

Take this week, for example. In the weeks leading up to my writing this book, I gave birth to my first child, with all the attendant joy and exhaustion. My mom arranged for a long stay near my husband and me in England, intending those first days to be a time of real Girls' Club support as she helped me to adapt to new parenthood, sharing the delight of the gift of a new person to our family. But after a forty-seven-hour labor and a snowstorm that made getting to the hospital pretty hard and meant the birthing center was closed, things got off to a hectic start. Within days of the birth, my mom fell and seriously injured her cornea, leaving her with incapacitating pain and a temporary loss of sight in her right eye. My sister, up to her eyeballs in PhD revisions, dropped everything to take a train from Scotland to see us but found she was pretty much in need of a break herself.

This is life, in its craziness and fear, its stress and splendor. But this is exactly where the Girls' Club kicked in, as the grace of our long friendship invaded the wrestle and wonder of this season in its difficulty. Not one of us had much to give, but we gave each other presence, hope, and a bit of laughter. We snatched hours to drink a cup of tea together, we spent quick moments in prayer for each other, we gathered to watch a movie when stress threatened to overwhelm all of us in different ways. We still discussed what we were reading (because we are incapable of not doing this). We pounded up and down the sidewalks between our houses—for a visit, a hug, a bite of something sweet, a few tears, an hour of commiseration. We took turns making meals, and we texted encouragement when one of us felt at the end of ourselves. We were present to each other, as we have been for years, in the topsy-turvy spectacle of life. We are the Girls' Club.

After all these years of cultivation, being friends is an old habit. But the richness of this time is rooted in decades of chosen close-ness, of willed, planned connection. We've invested time to talk when we lived thousands of miles apart; we've made space for trips together; we've created patterns of deep conversation, prayer, cele-bration, and forgiveness. These choices are the soil in which our present friendship is rooted. It's the soil we so hope you will learn to cultivate from the pages of this book. Whether you come to this book rich in a similar companionship or you come with an ache for such friendship, our hope is that as you read, you will discover the continual possibility of creating, nurturing, and initiating the kind of friendships that will endure in beauty and tenderness. We hope you find the same assurance in yourself that I knew even as an opinionated little two-year-old girl.

We're the girls. We're strong. We laugh. We do things together. We make light in the darkness. And after decades of friendship, I'll add one more: we always will.

JOY ℘ On January 17, 2018, Theresa May, the prime minister of the United Kingdom, announced the creation of a new position in the British government: the minister of loneliness. In her statement on the decision, May said, "For far too many people, loneliness is the sad reality of modern life."[1] Though the headline seems stranger than fiction, I think most of us read that and feel a twinge of resonance. Life, it seems, is lonely these days.

Though we live in a world with constant access to connection through social media, many of us walk around with a hollowness in our hearts, an unmet desire for connection. Despite the serious diagnosis of pervasive loneliness, friendship tends to be taken lightly. Popular portrayals seem frail, vapid, unimportant. Friendship is often thought of as a pleasant, inessential part of life—something we'd all like to have but can live without. Women's friendships in particular receive poor treatment, ranging from the sickeningly saccharine to overstated viciousness. We are furnished with stories like *Mean Girls*, *Sex and the City*, and *Girls*, which accomplish nothing more than putting a finger on the deep ache we feel when comparing the inadequacy of the friendships we have with the ones we can imagine.

I think most of us long for deeper relationships, but we are sometimes stymied as to how we should go about cultivating them. That desire for companionship is not frivolous; we are not meant to be alone. Social scientists have found that people who are isolated have a higher mortality rate and a lower life expectancy. And isolation has become more and more common in our society; the tight-knit communities that formed around things like locality or a vocation in agriculture that used to provide us with ready-made connections have dissolved. But the alternatives that our culture has offered us seem almost insulting. We are hungry for the sustenance of sturdy, deep friendships, but we are fed an idea of friendship that is neither nourishing nor satisfying.

Friendship can and must be so much more.

I was lucky, because I was born into a communion of potent friendships. I grew up as a member of the Girls' Club.

At its most basic, Girls' Club was simply my mother's way of ensuring little pockets of time with just my sister and me—no boys allowed. Whether it was an afternoon at a tea shop, an evening watching one of our favorite movies, or a trip, my mom made time for herself, my sister, and me, away from my brothers and dad, to bond, laugh, discuss, and dream together. We like the boys, even love them, but sometimes a girl just needs to be with her Girls' Club.

But there was also a purpose to these times together: to grow in friendship so we could become the fullest, bravest, and happiest women we could be. I remember our trips most vividly. They felt special, important, exciting. There was always a sense of intentionality and celebration. At some point along the way, my mother would turn to my sister and me with a sparkle in her eyes to unfold the plans for our special time together. It would include any special events planned (maybe a movie together or a concert), what food we might eat (a really essential part of any Girls' Club gathering), and usually some topic of conversation, contemplation, or dreaming that we would discuss together.

As we got older, Sarah and I contributed to the planning of these adventures, learning to love the healthy pride that comes with being the instigator in a friendship. In each season, from little girlhood to burgeoning womanhood to dizzying adulthood, Girls' Club was our place to dream, discuss, celebrate, and grow together as women.

Out of our friendship grew a culture of womanhood. I grew up thinking women were mighty and gentle, capable of feats of extraordinary bravery, thoughts of astounding depth, and quiet works of mercy. My picture of womanhood grew out of our sorority; it grew out of our friendship. My image of what friendship ought to be and what I ought to be as a woman grew out of the great cloud of mighty women who surrounded me.

Perhaps this is why I feel such wild discontentment with the state of friendship in our world.

I think that friendship is so much more colorful, crucial, and challenging than most people let it be. Our limited imaginations regarding friendship keep it pent up, restrained from bursting out of its gate and releasing its full power and beauty.

This book is concerned with the making and keeping of soul friends. We write it not only for you, reader, but for us, for me. I, too, have moments—months even—of loneliness. I am on the front lines with you, fighting for companionship.

With this book, we wish to pass on a vision for the power that friendship between women can generate and also to sketch some practical wisdom for cultivating these relationships. If nothing else, we hope to set your imagination free and to paint a picture of what richness and delight and depth friendship can hold. I think the best way we can give you this vision is by passing on the stories of the best and dearest friends in our lives. It is our great pleasure to tell these stories, and we hope they will encourage you and teach you the goodness and power of women's friendship.

CHAPTER 1

Commitment: The Glue That Preserves the Bond of Friendship

You don't fall into love. You commit to it.
Love is saying, "I will be there, no matter what."

TIM KELLER

Jonathan went to find David and encouraged him
to stay strong in his faith in God.

I SAMUEL 23:16

SALLY ⌘ It is often the small events in our lives that have big consequences. Yet in the flow of normal days, we are unaware that such events are about to occur. February 2, 1978, dawned just like any other day. I did not know that an inauspicious event on that day would change my life profoundly.

Having been challenged to consider investing my life in missions, I had a pathway open up for me to work in Communist Eastern Europe in 1977. My assignment would be to work on a traveling team that trained and discipled leaders in countries throughout the area, countries that were, at that time, under the control of Russia.

My entrance into this traveling life started when I found an apartment with two other girls in a small home in a district in Vienna near the vineyards, with the famous Vienna Woods nearby. Living on the top floor of an Austrian bungalow in a tiny room with a slanted roof meant that I could stand up to my full height in only one part of the room. That particular morning, I had crawled out of bed, rushed to grab a bite to eat in the shared kitchen with my roommates, caught the bus and then the tram, and ridden downtown for another morning of German at the Goethe institute of language.

Having arrived in Vienna six months before, I was thick into language training but still getting my feet wet in learning the culture of my new home. As a traveling missionary to Communist countries—Romania, Hungary, Yugoslavia, and Poland—I was studying German mainly to be able to live well inside Austria.

That evening I was looking forward to meeting a friend I had been corresponding with for a couple of months but had never met. Gwen was her name, and she had lived with a former roommate of mine, so I wanted to welcome her to Austria. We would be working together occasionally in this wild adventure of seeking to take the gospel behind the Iron Curtain with a team of others who were committed to the same task. She had visited for a few weeks at a summer student camp, but she had just moved to Austria for the long haul. I anticipated some tension in our relationship because my former roommate had said, "I don't think you two will get along at all. You are so extremely different from each other." This comment had prepared me for polite conversation but left me with low expectations for a close friendship.

It was Gwen's second official day in Austria after moving there full time. Since she naturally felt apprehension about finding her way around Vienna during the first week, I planned to meet her at a tram stop that intersected a busy street halfway between her home and mine. It would take both of us about half an hour to get to the meeting place. Since all the stops were announced in German and there was a hustle and bustle of people getting on and off, it was always a little precarious to figure out when to get on or off a bus or tram. I attempted to give her simple instructions and told her that I would be waiting at the stop.

The area where we would meet was still new to me, and I knew only enough German to begin getting around the city without getting lost. I could barely find my way around a grocery store, where all the words of food were new to me. Yet I wanted Gwen to think she was in good hands, so I clothed myself with an air of confidence as we both forayed into a new neighborhood.

Boot-clad, scarf-wound, wool-coated people swirled around me as I pushed my way through the exit door. I was hoping I had arrived first so I could flag Gwen down as she approached the island in the middle of the street where we would meet.

After five minutes of standing among the crowds in the chilly winter air, I peered into the dark night at a red tram gliding snake-like toward the crowded platform. Sure enough, it was number 37, the one I knew she would be riding.

I spotted a tall, chestnut-haired young woman sporting a red jacket. Her appearance resembled the photograph I had received from her, confirming that this was her. She looked very American amid the sea of dark coats that the Austrians generally wore. I waved energetically above the crowds to attract her attention. Relief danced through her eyes as we made eye contact and I ran to greet her.

The cold night air whooshed about us, and I looked around for a café where we could sit inside to eat and chat.

The word *Stüberl* was lit up in front of a tiny window across the street. I supposed it to be a neighborhood café, but in reality it was probably a local bar. Even so, I forged ahead, confidently holding Gwen's arm and guiding her through the crowd as though I knew what I was doing.

As we entered, we were accosted by the slight stench of smoke, and a faint brown haze hovered above the few tables in front of a bar filled with men gulping their beer. As the only women in the room, we felt the eyes of the strangers following our awkward movements, so we quickly sat at a little table in the corner as out of the way as we could manage. The only meal I recognized on the menu was goulash, so I ordered two, along with some sparkling apple juice (*apfelsaft gespritzt*).

We talked easily, and conversation began to fill up the spaces in our hearts. We hardly noticed that the greasy soup had finally been served because from the first, both of us were caught in the miracle of finding a kindred spirit in such an inauspicious place as a smoky little bar in a foreign country. We both had come to Austria in faith that God would meet us in this place. And so He had.

As the hours passed, Gwen and I were unaware of what was happening around us. Connecting on a spiritual level, immersed in deep, delightful conversation, we were oblivious to the comings and goings of the men in the room. Before me was a woman rich of soul because she had invested her life in serving others, studying Scripture, facilitating countless meetings in a college ministry, and teaching and leading young women. She had formed friendships with people from all over the world. To find the treasure of such rich companionship was a rare gift for me after lonely months of learning to be faithful alone in a foreign land. Our newfound friendship seemed a surprise gift from God.

Gwen's "excellent self" unearthed desires inside me to become my most excellent self. Her thoughts challenged me to become a more resilient student of great ideas. Her gentle love gave room for me to show my true self, warts and all.

Rare was my experience to find someone who would seek *me* out and delve into questions aimed lovingly at finding out my story, exploring my history, my fears, my passions. Having a friend reach into my own heart by enthusiastically pursuing me was an unusual experience, as I was so used to being the one to reach out, to keep conversations going.

Soon after that first meeting, I got a note from Gwen asking me to join her for dinner at her apartment. "Come in and sit for a while and let's be friends" were the most welcoming words I had heard in months. As I looked for her apartment number on the cozy old vine-covered building, she suddenly emerged from a hallway balcony and pointed. "This way!"

She was the first woman around my age in six months to actually invite me to her home for a meal. Yes, I had gone to language school; found my way around this strange new city, only getting lost about five times; and even learned how to buy groceries and shop at the outdoor markets with my very limited German, but I longed for a personal touch. Loneliness as I had never felt it thrummed through every beat of my heart. I wished for someone to talk to who understood the foreignness of being in a country where few people fluently spoke my native language.

I even remember what she served me that night—meatloaf, cottage cheese, and steamed broccoli. Not fancy, but it seemed so familiar from an American standpoint. I remember it as one of the best meals of my life because it was served with such kindness and love. She extended the hospitality of Jesus to me, and it warmed me to my toes.

From this humble evening, we decided to meet once a week. Before long, we were going to concerts together (music is the love language of Vienna, as it's the home of Mozart, Beethoven, and other famous musicians). When we had open weekends, we explored new mountain villages in the Alps and snacked on the train. In meeting often, we became like sisters. We did life together between our ministry trips, language study, and other commitments.

Eventually, Gwen moved to Poland to open our ministry there with another team. Before she left, we met at our favorite coffee spot. Our conversation flew to many subjects so we could get in everything we wanted to say before she would be in another country. At some point, and neither of us remembers how, we began to talk about Jonathan and David from the Bible. Theirs was a story of committed friendship. David had been chosen by God to become the king who would eventually lead all of Israel in their worship of God. We know from Acts that David was chosen because he was devoted to seek God, to follow Him, to love Him. We read in Acts 13:22, "God removed Saul and replaced him with David, a man about whom God said, 'I have found David son of Jesse, a man after my own heart. He will do everything I want him to do.'"

Perhaps in the context of David's anointing at such a young age, God provided a friend who would walk beside him for a while and help him sustain the challenging call on his life. Perhaps that's why He gave him Jonathan as a friend.

We read, "Now it came about when he had finished speaking

to Saul, that the soul of Jonathan was knit to the soul of David, and Jonathan loved him as himself" (1 Samuel 18:1, NASB). We pondered what it meant that Jonathan's soul was knit to the soul of David, and in the context of our conversation, we decided that God had knit our souls together. We made a sort of pledge to each other to support each other, to seek the other's good, to help when help was needed. We decided we would be friends for life.

We found another verse that reflected the foundation of David and Jonathan's friendship: "Jonathan went to find David and encouraged him to stay strong in his faith in God" (1 Samuel 23:16). This phrase became a sort of promise we made to each other to commit to helping each other stay strong in our faith as we walked with God. And as young women, we made a sincere promise to be friends for life and to uphold our commitment to help one another.

Eventually I was assigned to the same team as Gwen and moved to Poland, where we tried to establish a ministry in this Communist country. Learning to live in the shadow of Communist rule, with little food available, visits from the police, and challenges at every point forged a deeper understanding in our hearts of the sacrifice people all around us were making to follow Christ.

Daily life was demanding and lonely. But Gwen and I created a home that was a haven where others could find hot tea, warm bread and cheese, and a welcome from the darkness of life outside our walls. Eggs seemed to be the main protein we could find in the stores, as meat, along with vegetables and fruit, was scarce. Discovering new ways to cook eggs or making simple soups each evening provided a welcome reprieve in our challenging days. We lit candles, turned on music on our small tape recorders, and finished the evenings by reading books aloud together. Our sweet companionship became a beautiful reflection of the love of God to the many people who came to our fourth-floor walk-up apartment. We partnered together to teach Bible studies, to pray with the brokenhearted, and to usher others into an atmosphere of safety, comfort, and heartfelt compassion from Christ.

As I reflect on the deep friendship that began that night so many years ago, I can better understand how God provided us with what we both needed in order to find the strength to fulfill His call on our lives, even as He provided Jonathan for David. The care and support of godly friendship sustained us through the rigorous and demanding life of pursuing missions in Communist countries at the beginning of our friendship and as we pioneered new ministries through the years.

Now, forty years later, I understand that this treasure of friendship was, in a way, God's gift to me that would safeguard me from falling during the periods of darkness and temptation that would come through the years. When we lived in different countries, we supported each other through faithful letter writing, phone calls, and yearly visits. We bore each other's burdens as we faced the deaths of family members and the challenge of illnesses. Our friendship helped provide the spiritual strength to keep following hard after Christ as we lived faithfully through all dark and joyful seasons of life.

I could not have imagined on the first night we met how this amazing, quiet woman would become like a family member to me over forty years of companioning me through the trials and personal tests of my life.

After I moved away from Poland, I married and had four children. Our family was led to begin a ministry, start a publishing business, host conferences, write books to inspire others, and move seventeen times. Yet God had planned to provide me personally with a friend who would impart love, strength, a listening ear, a praying heart, and wise counsel through each new phase of life. He knew that a godly friend was what I would need to be able to pursue what He wanted us to do. When I lacked family support, Gwen loyally encouraged me, my husband, and my children as though we had been born sisters from the very start.

Later, as my husband and I engaged in a spiritual battle to help preserve families in a culture bent on destroying them, God knew we would need friends to walk beside us and to give us the strength to pursue His ideals against much opposition. Even as a single woman, Gwen always believed in the messages that burned in my heart, and she would share encouraging words, write notes of Scripture, share books to inspire me, and shower my children with the charming love of an "auntie" they otherwise would not have had.

Perhaps God plans to fulfill our deep needs for friendship so that we can better feel His love in a world where we hunger for companionship as we do His Kingdom work.

As I look back over the years, it occurs to me that the context for friendship, especially friendship in the Lord, is so important to keep us growing toward His desire for us to know Him intimately. God is always doing more than we can think or imagine, and even though the gift of a friend may seem like a wonderful personal gift, He always has more in mind. Spiritual friendships are not just about personal fulfillment but also about the scope and journey of what God wants to accomplish in our lives and how He wants us to live in His Kingdom ways. We could not do this without friends.

In a world where most people feel isolated, alone, unseen, and lonely, we need this view of friendship as something that shows us the fullness of God's love more than ever. To cherish and guard friendships can be a safeguard from personal pettiness and a reminder to be selfless. To embrace a friendship in full-fledged commitment provides us with a visible picture and personal experience of what we hope for in God: one who will love us, help us, and respond to us, no matter our failures, our needs, our vulnerabilities, or our prickly moments. It is a picture of a forever-and-always love that gives life.

As I look around, sometimes it feels like the fabric of society is falling apart—people are lonely, marriages are disintegrating, children do not know if they are wanted or loved, nothing in areas of ethics or morality can be counted on. The deadly effects of this cultural slide are painfully obvious—from the social and political implications of leaders falling to people in power abusing those in positions of weakness to the deeply personal pains of broken families. I think part of that destruction comes from people lacking godly support and friendly encouragement, from not having a cloud of witnesses surrounding them to spur them on to faithfulness in living out biblical ideals.

When we are devoid of the support or sympathy that comes from deep, close, loving relationships, we are more easily tempted to look for temporal things to fulfill our needs, to compromise our previous heartfelt commitment to follow hard after Christ. This kind of support—the accountability of godly friends—reminds us to be faithful in our own stories, to remember the legacy of believers who have gone before us.

God designed family, friendships, and church to help sustain us personally in following Him and serving Him. We were not created to handle the demands of life alone. Even as we would never send a soldier into battle without a battalion to give support and strength or an officer to provide leadership and wisdom, we should not be fighting our spiritual battles alone. Yet many believers have become so alienated in their lives, so isolated from real relationships, that they don't even perceive that they are failing to thrive. They don't know what they were designed to have—real people, real relationships, real accountability, real compassion, real help. That is why cultivating, cherishing, and nurturing godly friendships is not just a luxury but a necessity to be able to sustain a healthy spiritual life. Yet I realize that it was in making a commitment to be friends for life, choosing to love each other even when we were not lovable, and investing time even when it was demanding that we cemented our friendship together.

Gwen has been God's grace to me through all the journeys and battles of life. Through her, God taught me that life is not meant to be lived alone. She was God's answer to my deep ache for friendship. I pray every person gets to experience the richness of such a fellow traveler in life.

I don't know where you are on this journey of soul-level friendship. Perhaps you have had a David-and-Jonathan kind of friendship for years, or perhaps you find yourself living far away from your family and friends, or perhaps you have always longed for a kindred spirit. As we embark on these chapters together, I invite you to pray for a "Gwen" in your own life—someone whose soul God knits together with yours and whose mutual commitment will mean you will always have someone to be there for you through all your years.

CHAPTER 2

The Voice of Loneliness
and the Voice of Love

The most terrible poverty is loneliness and
the feeling of being unloved.

MOTHER TERESA

Perfect love casts out fear.

1 JOHN 4:18, NASB

SARAH ✎ Candlelight fluttered over the battered wood tables, the polished glasses, and the dim corners of my favorite French café in Oxford as my mom and I sat down to dinner. The evening outside was chill, but the little café was bright and cozy, with baguettes in a pile on our table and the pleasant thrumming of conversation beneath the skim of classical music. I loved this café; it was why I had chosen it as the place to take my mother when she came to see me during my first year of study.

Usually I savored the Paris-type feel of the tables pushed up close to each other, the friendly banter, the feeling that you could almost reach over and take a taste off your neighbor's plate. But

13

that night I wished us miles away, because the only thing my neighbors were going to get from our table was the extra salt from my splashing tears. I hadn't even known I needed to cry. But my mother arrived and asked a few searching questions, and the combination of candlelight, French bread, and sympathy was too much. Soon I was crying so hard I could barely get words out (and it didn't help that I was trying to be discreet while doing it). But once I did, I choked out the single fact of my woe.

"Mom, I'm just so lonely. Again."

The months leading up to that aggrieved moment had seemed so rich in the possibility of friendship, something I was starving to find. I had arrived in Oxford for a year of study just after my thirtieth birthday, and frankly, it felt like heaven. I came to that year abroad out of the just-finished and difficult decade of my twenties. I was itching for good work, for long-term friendships, for local community, for ministry. In the past several years I had struggled, as I think many in my generation do, to figure out where to put down roots, how to create lasting friendships, how to wrest community from what always felt like the huge, anonymous push of modern life. I traveled, I wrote, I worked for student ministries, I tried this church and that, always keeping an eye open (let us be honest) for that great romantic love I felt sure was out there somewhere. I looked for friends with similar ideals, with a love for literature, with a sense of mission driving their actions. But I found those friends to be few and far between, and as the years passed and I moved yet again or another community broke apart, frustration began to build. The prospect of a year in England, a country I loved for its literature and beauty, felt like the chance for a change with some freshened vision.

And oh, Oxford felt like the answer to all my prayers.

I arrived just as the leaves were turning and settled into a tiny turret room on the top story of an Oxford college, where I could watch pink sunrises blossom behind the cross on the chapel roof each morning. I shared a kitchen with students from all over the world, where we gathered after a day of classes for late-night feasts of toast and tea with philosophical talks on the side. My sister, in a different program, lived just on the other side of the rambling old house, and we sneaked out for coffee on Saturday mornings, both of us brimful with things we'd learned and new convictions to share. On my own, I walked cobblestone streets and soaked in the old, bookish beauty of golden-walled Oxford, I gloried in doctrine classes, and I mulled over my essays on C. S. Lewis while sipping tea in my favorite bookshop. I was part of a small, close-knit, lively community of students from around the world; there was always someone to talk to, a book to discuss, an evensong service to attend with the larger group. There was even a tall, charming Dutchman at my church with whom I shared a passionate interest in children's books and theology, who didn't seem averse to chatting about them whenever I was around. Oh yes, Oxford was heaven, and in those first sweet months, I was daily, blessedly happy. For the first time in years, I felt that I belonged.

And then, gradually—again—I didn't. Or rather, the old struggles began to seep into the glory of what I thought was a new life. The days grew long and dark, the streets cold, the pressure of intensive deadlines and essays hit hard, and the friends I had made began to have less time and a lot more stress. The big, merry kitchen group began to separate as our different programs demanded different commitments. The evenings got long and lonely. My sister moved back to the States. I began to wonder what in the world would follow this single year abroad, to face the fact that I had no visa or reason to stay when my essays were finished; my sense of belonging was an illusion. The Dutchman's spiritual adviser told him to consider the religious life of an Anglican monk (he did and then chose me instead, but that's another story, and it sure took a long time). My two bosom friends left for the long Easter break along with the rest of the college, and I suddenly found myself living alone in a tower room that felt like something in a gothic novel by one of the Brontës, a shadowy place that sat amid long, deserted corridors in a building emptied of human voices and light. I couldn't think of anyone to call. Or anyone who might call me. I met my mom that night after a week of deep isolation, in which I had worked nonstop to distract myself from my loneliness. But the touch of my mom's compassion opened my heart. When we got back to her bed-and-breakfast that night, propped up against a pile of pillows with a good stack of dark chocolate nearby, I finally managed to articulate my woes.

I was lonely. Deeply lonely. Again. Nothing had changed. Real, lasting friendship, a place to put down roots as a young adult— these still seemed beyond my grasp, and the fact that the old loneliness could follow me even to Oxford made me wonder if there was actually something wrong with me. I felt profoundly rejected, as if somehow the isolation I felt was personal. And I was afraid I always would.

I wonder if you have ever felt the same way.

In this book, which is largely a celebration of the warmth and camaraderie I have known in the Girls' Club with my mom and sister and in the feminine friendships that have shaped our lives, it feels odd to open with an exploration of loneliness. Surely, rich as I am in those core friendships, I should put the issue of loneliness aside—and the temptation to do so is great. Idealist that I am, I'm always in the business of happily-ever-afters. In movies, in marriage, in friendships, I hunger for the perfect, I focus on the beautiful, I celebrate what is possible, not what isn't. But when I look back over the past decade and more, over the deep wrestlings of soul I have known as a purpose-hungry twenty-something, as a single woman grappling with her identity and in search of love, as a newly married woman still dealing with the hunger for friendship, I am aware that loneliness has been one of the great companions and formative themes of my life.

Actually, this has been true for my mom and my sister as well, and I believe it's true for most women. Loneliness, and the way it makes us question whether we are lovable, is an issue that we in the Girls' Club have each had to face, because we have all known deep loneliness in our different spheres of life. Being the Girls' Club is a profound and beautiful gift, but it doesn't mean we haven't had to walk alone. In this broken world—as we foray forth to love and work, to look for friendship, to minister, to learn—we will come up again and again against our deep need for love, the imperfection of others, our longing for affirmation, our sense of perceived and sometimes real rejection. Because of this, I think we have no choice but to begin by talking about loneliness. It is, after all, the condition in which we are all seeking relationship, connection, and love.

Some of the greatest gifts of the Girls' Club have always been, first, a shared willingness to support each other through our breakdowns (a vastly important aspect of long-term friendship) and, second, a desire to help one another past the surface emotion to where the deep doubts and questions must be addressed. Throughout my life, my mom and sister have helped me to be honest: with the source of my emotion, with the way my own insecurity shapes my relationships, with the doubt I bear about God's love and how that influences my capacity to receive love from others. We love each other well in part by helping each other to get to the root of the pain that could easily lead us to more isolation. We ask the hard questions. We take a close look at the world. And we love each other best by pushing one another once more into the arms of the lover-God, whose business is the binding up of our broken hearts.

That's exactly what my mom did for me during that Oxford Easter break, and it's what I hope you will begin to do yourself through what we explore in this chapter. Emily Dickinson, that solitary, wistful poet, wrote that there is a "loneliness one dare not sound,"[1] and it sounds like good advice—at first. I spent many years trying to deal with loneliness that way, ignoring it and looking for friends, moving on to the next project or church in hope of some great love that would settle my fear of rejection for good. But I have come to believe that we must sound our loneliness, because if we don't, it will become the voice defining our sense of self, our security in our friendships, our understanding of God's grace towards us. Loneliness can quickly sabotage our very ability to reach out in friendship if we allow the insecurity it brings to define the way we relate. We have to acknowledge and resist it. We have to confront the daily habits and cultural patterns by which we are made lonely. Ultimately, we have to challenge the voice that speaks in our loneliness, challenging what it whispers to us about our worth.

My mom helped me to sound my loneliness in those quiet days we shared in Oxford, and that soul-searching was shaped by two questions. The first—*Why am I lonely?*—was one I needed to answer for myself. I needed to look at the patterns of my life, the cultural norms by which I was living, and ask myself how they shaped my capacity for relationship. The second question—*Am I lovable?*—was one that only God could answer. Only in learning to listen to the voice of love instead of the voice of loneliness was I able to begin to answer the voice in my head that told me I would never be loved.

Why Are We All So Lonely?

Just a few months before I began writing this book, I came across a headline in a major British newspaper: "Loneliness Is an Epidemic." Curious, I googled the headline and the term and found that various contemporary doctors, writers, psychologists, and politicians are increasingly aware of the way modern people feel isolated, unseen, and profoundly alone. As I read numerous articles, I began to wonder, *Are we lonelier than our ancestors?* What I have come to believe is that yes, we are. There are certainly spiritual and emotional causes of loneliness that are common to every generation, but there are also cultural factors that shape our experience of the world, helping or hindering our relationships with other people. If we are to confront and heal our loneliness, I think we have to deeply evaluate the cultural patterns that separate and isolate us. We live in an age that makes real-life friendship increasingly difficult because the patterns of modern life make us strangers to each other.

First, we are largely an uprooted society. Our mobile culture means we rarely know our next-door neighbors; we are no longer rooted to *place*, so we no longer have the instant and deep connection of a community bound to one another by a shared life in a single location. When I first encountered the writing of Wendell

Berry, a farmer and poet who writes in defense of rural communities and of the grace of being rooted in "a place on earth,"[2] I felt almost desperate to have the local life he described. I was ready to move to a farm for good if only it meant the possibility of belonging, of being deeply known and loved. But where would I move? What if there is no land to return to (like Wendell Berry's family farm)? What if God calls you somewhere else? My family moved twelve times before I was eighteen, always hoping to be able to settle for good, but that was never our story. It certainly hasn't been mine as an adult either. While there were always good and often ministry-driven reasons for the moves, they were also driven by jobs in different places, by a mobile world that required us to keep starting over. We were part of a larger cultural movement that means few people stay in one place and few people know their neighbors. The world is on the move these days, which means many of us have never known long-term, place-based, unconditional community.

Second, we are a distracted society living in a largely virtual world. We operate our daily lives increasingly in the presence of the internet, our screens drawing our attention and experiences away from the here and now into an anonymous, unresting, unrooted space. Social media provides connection of a kind, but it is no replacement for the gift of present, vulnerable, face-to-face friendship. What we portray online is an avatar of our true selves, a symbol we craft that stands in for us in the online universe. We have an immense amount of power in crafting it to reflect the best of what we are and what we love, but that also means we never present the fullness of ourselves—or receive it from anyone else. Nor can the sound bite of social media statements and opinions truly represent the depth and wonder and frailty of a real human being in person. The online world simply cannot offer us the intimacy of seeing someone at their best . . . and their worst, the grace of a friend's embodied hug, the wholeness of an actual person with all their foibles and unmatchable beauty.

The problem is that the internet, by its nature, is a profound distraction, one that draws our consciousness out of the real world and into the unending information of the virtual world. Complicating this is the fact that we often use the distraction of the online world to medicate the deep loneliness we feel; we can scroll through countless feeds, our phones the ever-present companions we wish we could find in real life. But there is a danger of so submerging our loneliness in distraction, of so immersing ourselves in the virtual that we become incapable of hungering for—and reaching out to grasp—true relationship. The fact that loneliness has become an epidemic in the internet age is no coincidence.

When online distraction is combined with the anonymity of the restless modern world, when we do not even know our neighbors and live far from family, when the online facades we create keep us from being truly known in both our ordinary glory and our brokenness, when our sense of isolation is so great that we immerse ourselves in busyness, we become part of a world where loneliness is, indeed, epidemic. We are pervasively, existentially lonely, and I think it is important to recognize that reality in our frenetic age. Are we lonelier today than the generations before us? Yes, in a way, we are. We live in a profoundly individualistic world, one whose modes of work, entertainment, and information train us to increasing isolation. We have to understand this and own the influence it has on our relationships if we are ever to live in gentle, intentional defiance of those patterns, confronting our loneliness and learning how to fight for the creation and maintenance of true friendship.

Much of what you will find in the pages that follow are the practices of holy rebellion that we in the Girls' Club have learned to live by as we combat the isolating patterns of life in a far-too-busy world. It's a work of constant reevaluation as we repeatedly examine our lives, our habits, our exhaustion, asking ourselves how we can step out of a frenzied loneliness and into a present connection, whether that's a phone call to each other, a cup of tea with a friend, a summer away from Facebook, or the initiation of a local book club.

During the days following my mom's visit to Oxford, I weaned myself from the online world that had distracted me from my sense of isolation, and I made myself, yet once more, try an in-person Bible study at church. I mustered my introverted courage and resolved to ask a new person out to coffee each week. I knocked on the door of my neighbor down the dorm room hall, and I scheduled Skype dates with my siblings. Crucially, I also banned myself from early morning time online and became more diligent about my times of prayer, of early quiet, of Scripture reading. It was those early morning spaces that helped me to answer the second question more fully than ever before.

Am I Lovable?

Loneliness is a fundamental reality of the human condition. The problem of loneliness is as old as Eden, etched into the very fabric of what it means to be fallen human beings. We are lonely because we live in this broken place, separated from God and each other by sin and sorrow, by grief and struggle. Loneliness is a theological problem, and it's one that each of us has to face for ourselves. We have to delve deep into our core beliefs—about ourselves, about grace, about God's love and our worth—if we are ever to be people capable of giving love, as well as receiving it.

In my first year of studying theology, I was fascinated to find that loneliness is the way several theologians describe the result of sin. In the beginning—in God's perfect beginning—we were created to live in unbroken harmony with our Creator and with each other, giving our hearts and selves fully to each other, knowing each other wholly. Sin meant a total break in that joyous relationship. In theological terms, sin is actually defined as *incurvatus in se*, the self turned inward upon itself, seeking only its own gain instead of living outwards in love and connection with others. The fallenness of the world means that each of us experiences an essential loneliness, a deep sense of separation from each other, of being isolated and even unlovable. Ultimately, what we grieve is separation from the love that created us. Of course we are lonely.

We are also healed of that fundamental loneliness in Christ. He is the divine Lover whose gift of Himself to humankind healed our isolation and drew us back into fellowship. The whole gospel is, in its way, the tale of loneliness being turned backwards, of isolation defeated by the very presence of the God who is now with us. But this is one more of those now-and-not-yet realities that come with the fact that we are redeemed and healed in Christ, and yet . . . we still live in the broken place. Loneliness is still pervasive in human experience because until Christ returns, we'll continue to live in this fallen world, where sin and suffering have shaped the whole of human life.

The voice we hear naturally in our hearts is one of condemnation: *You're impossible to love. You're too difficult. You'll always be lonely. You're not worth attention.* And often that voice has been affirmed by the rejection or hatred we have known in the broken relationships of our lives. We bring deep wounds to our attempts at friendship, wounds that create an inner narrative of profound insecurity. What does that look like? For me, a series of petty friends and group rejection meant an increasing sense of doubt about my own worth that made every interaction with a possible new friend a torture. Even as I sought to connect, I was battered by an inner sense that I was ugly or ridiculous, that I'd said the wrong thing, that the other person found me too quiet, too wordy, too— well, it could be any number of things. Insecurity meant that every conversation became a space in which I was asking someone to answer the question "Am I lovable?" But no human could sufficiently answer that question, because I had already judged myself unworthy.

Those voices of loneliness are just one aspect of a fallen world working its hurt deeply into our lives. The difference—now that Christ has come into the world, his love kindling right amid the darkness in our hearts—is that loneliness no longer has the final word. Love has a new story to tell us, one that can define the whole of our existence and renew our capacity for relationship. The catch is that we have to learn to listen for the voice of love as it speaks healing into our hearts, calling us out of isolation and into our identity as those who are deeply beloved.

During the quiet days of my spring break in Oxford, after my mom left and I was again alone, I began to read Marilynne Robinson's novel *Lila*, and it became for me an image of what it looks like to listen to the voice of love crying out in the darkness of our hearts. *Lila* is the companion to the novel *Gilead*, a collection of letters written by an elderly pastor in small-town Iowa to the young son whose adulthood he knows he will not live to see. Lila, mother of that son, glimmers in the background of *Gilead*. We know, from the old man's words, that his marriage was late and startling, if not scandalous, to the small town and flock in his keeping. We also know that Lila had been a drifter, a rough woman with an unknown past.

In the novel *Lila*, we are taken into Lila's mind, seeing the story, the marriage, the coming child through her own eyes. In a masterful stream of narrative, in which Lila's thoughts leap between memory and present, past event and current meaning, we encounter not just a story but the shape of a mind that has been molded by loneliness, by suspicion, by a long, hard life on the road. Lila's inner voice is inclined to distrust everyone, and yet . . . she yearns to trust. We witness Lila's transformation through her hunger for love, her fragile hope in the gentle love of a good old man whose faithfulness has challenged the narrative by which she lives.

In many ways *Lila* is the story of two inner voices—that of loneliness and that of love—and the way they wrestle for primacy within Lila's heart. What gripped me as I read the novel was how familiar these voices were. As I read Lila's thoughts—thought them with her, really—I was startled by my initial inclination to believe Lila's inner narrative precisely because mine is often the same. I know the power of loneliness to tinge any offer of love with doubt, to steal away the innocence of joy, to darken the expectation of good. Lila's inner voice says things like this:

"You best keep to yourself, except you never can."[3] Loneliness tells her that it's dangerous to trust someone else, that isolation is safe. Loneliness always sets the painful past as a backdrop in Lila's mind so that her heart is tense and defensive.

"There were words so terrible you heard them with your whole body. *Guilty.* And there were voices to say them."[4] Loneliness heaps up every rejection she has known, every bad thing she's done, and tells her that this is the only thing that will ever be true of her.

"She had told herself more than once not to call it loneliness, since it wasn't any different from one year to the next, it was just how her body felt, like hungry or tired, except it was always there, always the same."[5] Loneliness tells Lila to stop hoping; it shows her the long line of people who left her, forgot her, and rejected her and presents those incidents as defining evidence of her worth as a person. And she believes that inner voice. She believes it so strongly that she almost cannot accept the love that comes to challenge the tyrannical finality of loneliness. And Lila's impulse is always to leave because she only feels safe in isolation.

But what about love, the voice that challenges that of loneliness? In the novel, love finds Lila in the form of the old man whose care both for her soul and for her heart is tenacious, long-suffering, and tender. The old man, even amid his own frailty and need, embodies that paean of love in 1 Corinthians, rooted as he is in a lifelong journey toward the healing love of God himself. What does the voice of love sound like? Love draws us into the present. Love draws Lila from the mist of her grief and guilt, summoning her to stand in the presence, not of phantoms, but of a human being whose hands and heart are offered to her.

"If the Lord is more gracious than any of us can begin to imagine, and I'm sure He is, then your Doll [Lila's sort-of guardian] and a whole lot of people are safe, and warm, and very happy. And probably a little bit surprised."[6] The old man saw a wholeness and hope for Lila that she could not see for herself. Love sees the beauty in Lila's loyal, suspicious heart and draws her, step-by-step, into health.

"If we stay here, soon enough it will be you sitting at the table, and me, I don't know, cooking something, and the snow flying, and the old man so glad we're here he'll be off in his study praying about it. And geraniums in the window. Red ones."[7] Love teaches us to hope, to see what is possible, to imagine beauty where there has been only grief.

"When you're scalded, touch hurts, it makes no difference if it's kindly meant."[8] Love is patient, and it hopes with a mighty will, because it takes a while for a hurt person to heal. It's a precious thing to watch hope grow in Lila's mind, to watch the faithfulness of love nurse her back to relationship.

"There was no way to abandon guilt, no decent way to disown it. All the tangles and knots of bitterness and desperation and fear had to be pitied. No, better, grace had to fall over them."[9] Grace must fall over us, too, over all the rejections we remember, the isolation we've known, the faithlessness that has wounded us to our core. Grace has to fall over our existential sense of loneliness, that constant human fear of being unloved. Grace has to invade the loveless patterns of a too-busy society. The only love that can really do that is the love of Christ, and that is why I think we have to begin talking about friendship by talking about our loneliness, because it is often the greatest hindrance to relationship. In order to have friends, we have to first learn what it means to *be* a friend, and we do that by being loved by God.

Only the loved can love—I heard that phrase in a talk many years ago and remembered it again as I read *Lila* and began to confront my own inner voice of loneliness. I decided to address that voice head-on, so I began by journaling through my fears of rejection, my sense of insecurity. I articulated my worst fears and found that suddenly, on paper, they were manageable, even frail, as

I began to read and memorize the powerful affirmations of God's love found in Scripture. I also read Julian of Norwich's *Revelations of Divine Love* and filled my imagination with powerful images of Christ's tender goodness. I sought counseling for some of the hurts that had twisted and shaped me toward fear over the years. I began to learn that sometimes I have to open wounds to let them heal, and the process was profoundly hopeful. Little by little, with the help of my family, of mentors, of a local church, I began to do what a mentor of mine once humorously said: "You can't just listen to your thoughts; you have to talk back to them!"

I began to live by the voice of love.

When we know that we are loved, we are ready to not just find a friend, but to be one. That's why we begin with our loneliness. In the silence of our fear, our need, our unmet hope, we face the worst. But a still, small voice sounds even there, the one voice that can set our hungry hearts at rest, the voice that teaches us how to be the friends and companions we so desire to find. And that's where real friendship begins. It's the only place it can.

CHAPTER 3

Learning to Embrace the Capaciousness of Womanhood

*In each of my friends there is something that
only some other friend can fully bring out.
By myself I am not large enough to call the
whole man into activity; I want other lights
than my own to show all his facets.*

C. S. LEWIS

JOY ✱ We had been walking a very long time. Much longer,
if we were honest, than any of us had wanted. The day had started
off beautifully.

My mom was intentional about making special times to be
with just us girls. My mother was intentional about everything,
including alone time with my brothers, so this was not surpris-
ing. Whether it was a trip downtown to eat a croissant and walk
around the beautiful Victorian houses (and imagine which one *we*
would want to live in); or an evening in eating popcorn, watching *Pride and Prejudice*, and deciding whether or not we actually
liked Mr. Darcy; or an afternoon making gallons and gallons of

applesauce to save for the winter, we had many moments through-out the months and years that were marked out for just us girls.

And once a year or so, we had a Girls' Club adventure.

Sometimes it was simply a night away somewhere close, but this year it was a real adventure: a week on Prince Edward Island, the birthplace of Anne of Green Gables, one of our most beloved literary heroines. It was the first Girls' Club trip I remember in detail. I was ten years old, and I remember because I was exactly one year younger than Anne in *Anne of Green Gables*, the book I was reading in preparation for our time there. First, we went to a speaking engagement with my mother. Being the extrovert that I was, I sort of liked walking around with my mother, speaking with people, and being charming. But once we packed up the books and shook every hand good-bye, we were on to the real business: exploring Anne's island!

That morning we had eaten our fill of the bed-and-breakfast's delectable spread (in all my traveling, I don't think I've ever had better food than at that little B and B!) and talked about plans for our day. We had heard that the inspiration for the White Sands Hotel (which features prominently in the Avonlea stories) was not too far away. We thought we might walk there for an early lunch. It was such a beautiful day! So we finished our breakfast and headed to the concierge.

"How do you get to the White Sands Hotel?" we asked.

"Oh! It's not too far," answered the kind Canadian concierge, with an accent reminiscent of another time. "Just four kilometers or so."

We were well fed and ready for a jaunt, so four kilometers sounded like nothing. The concierge pointed us in the right direc-tion, and we set off.

Oh, it was beautiful. It was June, and wildflowers were thick in every ditch. The sky was blue that day, but it was never too warm—perfect for me, as I wilt like a tulip in any temperature above seventy-five degrees. But the air that day was cool and pungent, with the fragrance of burgeoning life in every nook and cranny of the earth. We chatted and chirped as we marched on our way, taking in the fresh loveliness of it all.

We were having such a good time that we hardly bothered to wonder how long we had been walking, when suddenly it occurred to us that we'd been on our feet for quite some time. We wondered aloud whether we'd missed a turn. It was proposed that maybe we hadn't walked as far as we thought; my little ten-year-old legs might have been slowing us down.

We stopped the next people we passed on the trail and asked if we'd missed the turn.

"Oh, no!" said the wife. "You just haven't gotten there yet."

"It's about four kilometers up that way," her husband added.

We thanked them and kept walking. *Four kilometers to go?* It was only supposed to be four kilometers total! Something seemed off. But with the encouragement that we were on the right path, we kept walking. At least we had a beautiful view, Sarah remarked. And she was right . . . for a while. Ten minutes after that comment, however, the trail disappeared, and we found ourselves on a small path of pebbles next to a two-lane highway. We walked in a single-file line. Every few minutes, a car would rush by, sending our hair into a panic as the wind tossed it around. We tried to talk, shouting back and forth in our little queue. But then one person wouldn't hear, and we'd have to shout it four times for the other person to catch it, replacing the initial delight of sharing with an objectless annoyance. So eventually we fell into silence.

At that point, we'd been walking twice as long as we had been when we ran into the couple on the path. About two miles earlier, we'd lost hope of actually finding the hotel for lunch. All we wanted was some sign of civilization or a house whose phone we could borrow to call a taxi. Anything.

Instead, we saw acres and acres of fields.

What had started off as charming and beautiful began to seem a teasing monotony. Surely someone lived out here! Didn't someone own all this land? It appeared not.

Then, it came: hanger.

I should note at this point that I have notoriously bad blood sugar. If I don't eat something every two to three hours, my blood sugar begins to drop and then plummet and then bottom out. This usually results in shakiness and sometimes fainting, but most often, if I'm honest, a cloud of furious annoyance with the world and all its inhabitants. The moment when my blood sugar levels could have been easily repaired had long passed. My face was hot, and my footsteps were heavy.

"How long are we going to walk?" I demanded. I knew, being a perceptive child, that this detour was not planned and that my mother knew no better than I how long we would have to walk. But I was tired and hungry and wanted to vent my frustration to someone.

"I'm so sorry, honey. I think the man at the desk must have gotten his directions wrong," my mother said, genuine sympathy on her face.

"Well, I guess so!" I dramatically stomped my foot, causing a cloud of dust to emerge from the gravel. "I just can't walk much longer! I'm hungry and tired, and I think I'm getting a sunburn."

I watched the prospect of hitchhiking pass through my mother's eyes.

No! Not with my two daughters, her resolute eyebrows seemed to say. My mother is the consummate caretaker; there has never been a need she hasn't provided for. This situation challenged her desire to help us. Oh, wasn't there a way to fix this?

"We really have been walking forever, haven't we?" my mother said with a laugh. Her smile was a little dampened but mirthful nonetheless. "I wish I could change this, but I can't. But you know what? I think you have it in you to be brave."

In my present purposeless rage, all this talk sounded like pacification. I was not pleased.

Sarah chimed in, "You're like Anne of Green Gables. You've got an adventurous spirit."

This worked on me—I'm a sucker for Anne. I would have done anything to please Anne . . . even walk a picket fence. I began to perk up.

"Do you think you can walk a little farther with me?" my mother said.

I supposed I could. "Anne could, so I can."

I gathered my courage and stomped determinedly on. A few minutes later, we saw it! A blessed sign: "White Sands Hotel," with an arrow pointing up a winding road. We walked along it for another (yes!) fifteen minutes, and then we finally turned the corner and saw it: the White Sands! It stood regal and surprisingly stately in this middle-of-nowhere field. We all but ran to the hotel, trying to preserve our dignity.

And, at last, we ate. Oh, how wonderful to eat! I distinctly remember that I ate three sliders, which seemed infinitely more delicious and filling than if I'd had just one hamburger. Once we'd eaten, we began to take in the grandeur of the hotel. There were rich red carpets everywhere, and all the waitstaff dressed as if they were living in the 1890s. Someone gave us a tour, and I held my head high the way I thought Anne might and imagined that I was very refined indeed.

Even after all that walking, Sarah and Mom wanted to explore the gardens and walk around the forested pond. I was a bit exasperated, but that soon turned to curiosity and then reverie as I discovered my new fascination: a bleeding heart flower. It was bright and lovely . . . and what a name! I began to compose a tragic love story surrounding a bleeding heart.

When we'd had our fill of the gardens, we had the concierge call us a taxi. Sarah gestured covertly at the odometer. We counted the kilometers and then translated them into miles.

Twelve miles.

My mom was right. I did have it in me to be brave. I just needed someone else to call that out in me.

What Women Can Do

That walk on Prince Edward Island is a lot like life. Like that day, I've found that life usually requires more of us than we expect. More effort, more tears, more bravery, more endurance, more ingenuity than we knew to come equipped with. But I've also learned that I am stronger than I think, that there are reserves of energy and endurance that I can access if I just decide not to give up. When my mother looked into my eyes that day and told me she knew I could walk a little farther, she set a tone for my life. *You are capable of more than you know. You are the right one to handle your life. And what is more, you are never alone in the journey. You have your Girls' Club around you, and more fundamentally than that, you have God.*

I think you have it in you to go a little bit farther.

This year, my Girls' Club has given me the same message under different circumstances with higher stakes. I started my PhD this year. Just like the walk to the White Sands, it seemed like a challenge but a manageable one. What I couldn't have bargained for was the onslaught of loneliness after my three best friends moved away, the awkwardness of trying to figure out if I was doing this doctoral research right, the unexpected injury of my mom's eye, the wondrous interruption of my niece Lilian's birth. All of it left me dizzy, tired, overwhelmed. This year has been more than I bargained for.

Recently I called my mom on the phone. I had had quite enough of being an adult. I had wilted. I loved my research, I felt called to teach, mentor, and guide college students. Up to that point, I had worked hard, but I had never encountered anything that seemed insurmountable. But in that moment, I genuinely wondered, *Can I do this? Am I enough?*

I poured out my heart to my mom on the phone. She listened. She empathized. And then she said, "Joy. You have borne so much. I'm so sorry this year has been difficult. But I'm not worried about you. The Lord will take care of you. I see your roots growing deep. If you press into this season, trust God, and keep going, I think you will see the fruit of it."

In other words, she said again, *I think you have it in you to go a little bit farther.*

And I did.

It reminds me of a surprisingly profound line from a Winnie the Pooh cartoon: "There's something you must remember . . . You're braver than you believe, and stronger than you seem, and smarter than you think."

One of the greatest gifts of female friendship in my life has been that women have called out the strength in me that I didn't know I possessed and helped me rise to the occasion of life. Female friendship has been at the core of all societies for this very reason. There is a fierceness and a flexibility in womanhood, an ability to overcome despite insurmountable odds. Patient, clever eyes, looking for a way to make things work, to stitch life together like a colorful quilt made out of scraps.

Clarkson women. Those words hold a whole world of meaning for me. Let me try to give you a peek inside.

Clarkson women means queens of celebration. Every year we have a Christmas tea for all our friends. I picture the three of us, hard at work in our kitchen. I'm chopping grapes and pecans for our famous chicken salad, Sarah is straining raspberries for the raspberry soup. Mom is tossing the scone mixture together. We're all laughing and talking over the hum of activity. Sarah tells me about a Wendell Berry novel she's just read; I tell her about an indie artist I've just discovered; Mom reminds us that we have ten minutes till everyone arrives. Once every delectable item of food has been tucked in the bowl or oven where it belongs, we survey our work. The table is resplendent with colorful napkins and sparkling goblets. And then we survey ourselves. Oh! Just one last touch: lipstick!

When the guests arrive, we welcome them into our home, taking coats, laughing, asking questions, showing them where their seats are at the table, and assuring them wordlessly that they belong in our hearts and home.

To be a Clarkson woman is to be hospitable. Not in a picture-perfect magazine way, but in a "make people know they're loved and welcome, and feed them delicious food" way. Clarkson women know that when you prepare for someone's arrival, look them in the eye while welcoming them, and serve them a delicious meal, you're saying, "You're important. Interesting. Worthwhile. And you are loved."

And that is important to the Clarkson women.

Let me describe another scene.

It's the quiet hours of the morning, just after seven o'clock. It is Christmas break, and everyone is home. I must have tea and pray before I interact with humans every morning—the consequences are dire if I don't. So I slip out my door and head downstairs to snatch my cup of tea before the flood of other humans descends.

In the living room at the bottom of the stairs, I see my mama curled up on the green couch. All the candles are lit, and there's a gentle melody wafting out of her portable speaker. She used to have a big, blue "quiet-time chair," as she called it, but now the green couch has taken its place. Over our seventeen moves as a family, she always had such a spot, and we kids knew it was holy. Not to be disturbed. We began to want such a place ourselves.

She always sits somewhere where she can see out into the world. At our current home, her spot looks out on a little patch of pine forest. In the winter, a white blanket of snow covers the front yard. In the springtime, flowers peek through the window, reminding her that warmer days have come once again. She is gazing out on the beauty contemplatively, her Bible resting on her knees, a pen in one hand and a delicate teacup in the other. She hears me. She knows the routine, because she feels the same. She reaches out her hand, and I squeeze it. Then I head to make my tea, leaving her to pray and think on her own.

With my tea in hand, I make it up to my room. I, too, light my candles and put on quiet music. I sit down and take my first refreshing sip. Ah! I already feel more ready to face the day. I open my daily prayer book.

In the name of the Father, the Son, and the Holy Spirit. . . .

One thing I have asked of the Lord, and this is what I seek,

That I may dwell in the house of the Lord and seek him in his temple . . .

I read the words—the Scriptures and the reflections. I pray about my own little trials and tribulations and for the people I love and the people I'm trying hard to love. I ask for grace for the day. I take my last sip of tea and head downstairs. As I step out my door, Sarah's swings open. She's been doing the same thing.

Clarkson women love God. Even as we have our own independent relationships with God, our own patterns of prayer and quiet time, we are all supportive of each other in that walk. We share what we're learning; we pray for each other. We do not let our time go to waste.

Another example.

It's nine o'clock on a Tuesday morning. My mom and I are both a little bleary eyed, but we have cappuccinos and a cheesy egg quesadilla to split, so we'll be just fine. I'm home on a "break" from my PhD (is there ever a break in PhDs?), and mom is two weeks away from another book launch. We must work, but why not work together? We munch on our delectable breakfast and talk about morning things and life. (Have you noticed Clarksons are always eating? We truly are.) Once we're finished, we share a significant look: it's time!

We both pull out our computers and begin to type away,

Mom on her press emails for the launch, and me on tedious edits to my chapter.

After a while, I pull off one of my earbuds. "Do you think it's a two cappuccino morning?" I ask. "I'll buy."

I can tell by the impish look in my mom's eyes that it is. I order our second round and check in with Mom. How is it going? Will her to-do list ever be finished? How does she feel about the launch?

She checks in with me, too. Were my adviser's comments helpful? When did I think I'd submit my thesis? What's the next step?

Work is important to the Clarkson women. Meaningful, excellent, purposeful work. That looks different for us at different seasons. Right now my work is hard, long hours of study on my PhD so I can master a topic and learn to teach and mentor college students. My mom, in addition to writing books, is preparing talks for conferences. She calls me and says, "Oh, Joy! I don't want to just do this off the cuff. I want to give them something worthwhile." So she labors away at achieving excellence in her speaking. But right now for Sarah, "work" looks different. She is still writing, yes, and doing a marvelous job of it. But for the most part, her life is taken over at present with the work of loving her little daughter, Lilian. In these intense early months, Sarah's new job is as steward of all Lilian's affairs and gardener of her little soul, sowing love and attention there. And oh, what good work it is!

Clarksons have a high capacity for accomplishment, for excellence, for leaving their mark—whatever the calling, profession, or task may be.

I could give so many other examples of what it means to be a Clarkson woman. Clarkson women care for people in need, be it physically, emotionally, or spiritually. Clarkson women travel and experience new things. Clarkson women make it through hard times. Clarkson women always wear lipstick.

Growing up in the context of these friendships profoundly shaped who I am as a woman today. I am eleven years younger than Sarah, but I was always accepted full-heartedly into our cohort. As I looked around me, I saw such a capacious vision of what women *could* be.

Sometimes we are limited by what we think we, as women, *should* be. Pondering what you should be always comes with limits, because it implies a *should not*. But as I looked at my mom and my sister and the women I grew up knowing and loving—Gwen, Lynn, Sandra, Beth, Brandee, and so many more—I believed women were capable of just about anything. They could cook, sing, light candles, and be mistresses of domains that made others feel loved and welcome.

They could think well and work hard, bringing insights through their study, innovation through their work, and accomplishments through their dedication.

They could teach—academically, spiritually, and socially—guiding people into the subtle strength of which women are such skilled masters.

They could nurture life, with their bodies and their whole beings. They could give more than they thought they had to love, teach, train, and guide children, both their own and the spiritual children God gave them to love along the way.

They could do brave, scary things. They could endure more sorrow than seemed humanly possible. They could celebrate like no one else could.

They could use their bodies—in gardening, in running marathons, in skillful dance.

Women could, it seemed, do just about anything. And their gender didn't diminish their skill or grace—no! It added to it. People have sometimes asked me if I feel pressured to accomplish a lot or be excellent or live up to my family's "standards" (whatever that means to them!). And I can honestly say I do not. Rather than a *should* that might make me feel guilty or pressured or inadequate, our family had a *could* that helped me imagine all that I could be. And with that robust vision ahead of me, how could I not want to live into it?

Girls' Club set a culture of womanhood that I could live into, rather than be forced to fit into. And that, I think, is one of the powers of intentional, life-giving female friendship.

I think women are marvelous, and I love being a woman. I also think this is an incredibly confusing time to figure out what it means to live well in that identity. It can be confusing to know how to own our strength and power while also letting ourselves be gentle and vulnerable. It can be difficult to know what to want when the world seems to sell us only two very limited life packages: one of career and one of family. I think this vision of womanhood is incomplete. In my life, I have been lucky to be surrounded by a great throng of mighty women. They are multifaceted—they think, they feast, they create, they laugh, they give life with their bodies and with their kindness and generosity. When I look to them, I see that there is a capaciousness to womanhood. An ability to hold many things together.

I think we women need to embrace that capaciousness.

Living in the context of vibrant female friendships that show us the *could* of being a woman helps broaden our imaginations, push us forward, and support us along the way.

I have felt the power of this legacy more keenly than ever since the arrival of my niece, Lilian. She is a wonder. So complete, so small, so burgeoning with potential. When I look into her searching blue eyes, I am filled with wonder and an urgent sense of desire. I want to be a better woman, to walk this path of life well beside her, to point her towards God's fingerprints and kindness, to live a full, abundant life so that she, too, can know that she is free to live into hers.

I think I can express this best in a letter I wrote.

Dear Lily,

Welcome to the Girls' Club! We've been waiting for you for a long time now. We're so happy you've joined us!

The first thing to know is this: you are so loved! We don't really know what you will be like yet. At the moment you are all gurgles and smiles and wide eyes. We don't even know what color your eyes will be at the moment. But someday soon your personality will start to bloom.

What will you be like? Will you love words? Talking, writing, spinning tales, and finding truth? Or maybe you will prefer to use your hands and your body. Maybe you will love to run and dig and cook. Will you be quiet or loud? Academic or artistic? Scientific or a lover of song? Whoever you will be, I already love it, and so do your mama and my mama. There is already space for you, and plenty of it!

We want you to be all you can be. Oh! It fills me with wonder to imagine what your life might be like. I already know you will be strong, because you come from a long line of strong women. You can use that strength in so many ways; you can accomplish great things. You can be kind to people who make you want to be angry and mean. You can bear the sorrows of others. You can teach and know and write.

You can make it through things that are harder than you can even imagine. I hate to think about it, but I know troubles will come to you because they come to all of us. But when they come, I know you'll be all right. Because if we can, we'll be there for you. To hug you, to catch your tears, to advise you, to cheer you on as you pick yourself up. And if ever we can't be beside you, know this: the source of the love we share is always with you. God is always with you, and whatever goodness we share in friendship is preserved in God. It's like your mama says to me: we are held by God. We are safe. He holds our love. He will always hold you.

Lily, we are all so very for you! Whoever God has made you to be, we want to watch you soar. There are so many things you could be, and we are so excited to support you and love you along the way to be all that you will be. Just imagine the story God will tell with your life!

I can't wait to teach you the ways of the Clarkson women. Early morning quiet times. Big feasts. Great minds. Tender hearts. Girls' Club adventures. And always, lipstick.

We love you, dear heart.

Welcome to the club.

Auntie Joy

And, friend, I welcome you to the Girls' Club too. You were already a part of it anyway, but it's always nice to receive an official invitation. Whether you were lucky like me and grew up with a throng of mighty women around you or whether you are blazing the trail on your own, starting the legacy of love for yourself, you are a part of a long history of women who have done their best to love and to live well. You, too, can live into the capaciousness of womanhood and call other women to do the same. Whatever your history, you belong. Whatever your personality, preferences, worries, and warts, you have a lifetime membership. We are bonded together by God's love—that wonderful power that made and loves us all. We are the Girls' Club.

Welcome.

CHAPTER 4

Loving Each Other's Woundedness

A friend is someone who sings your heart's song back to you when you have forgotten the words.

DAVID COPPOLA

SALLY ✑ That Sunday, the early morning hours of a golden fall day presented a celebration of the art of God. It was one of those glorious days that you want to hold on to forever. Gorgeous foliage sang over my soul with brightest reds, blazing golds, and deep maroons, as cool, friendly breezes bespoke the soon-coming snows. Downtown Colorado Springs, with its blocks of turn-of-the-century Victorian homes, all bedecked with broad porches, spoke of earlier times. One could imagine that hours upon hours had been whiled away with children playing, grown-ups catching their breath and sharing the events of days spent at home and in family labor while marveling at the sunset against the backdrop of Pike's Peak.

I was walking slowly, meandering along these remnants of eight or ten blocks and enjoying the reverie that comes from such a day. Only there was one thing missing—the companionship of my dearest Sarah. Almost palpable was my longing for her to be beside me as she had been for at least a decade.

For many years, we had awakened at 6:30 on Saturday and sometimes Sunday mornings, before anyone else in the house stirred, to steal away together to our favorite downtown café, a haven for sharing secrets, discussing the profound ideas we had been pondering, and connecting to each other's soul dreams. Most of the year, when the weather allowed, we would follow our rendezvous with an invigorating walk in these wonderful porch-bedecked, tree-lined streets that whispered of over a hundred years of memories from families dwelling together, sharing life over the last century.

We loved these walks, and especially these blocks, because they reminded our hearts of the kind of community we can only dream of in this contemporary isolationist life—the neighborly relationships found in the world of Anne of Green Gables. The times when families lived close, neighbors knew each other and shared values and beliefs and life together, where children played freely in the gardens of each other's families while the adults befriended each other through the years. This was always the dream era that Sarah and I wished we had experienced firsthand. This became the place of sharing in each other's dreams and wishes and hopes.

Though we never experienced this kind of community in our real lives, we knew that there was something of great value in groups of people who cultivated life, love, and friendship in the context of living near one another through different seasons of life. And so we fanned the flame of these thoughts, and even though we could not shape our lives to create this experience, we were inspired to keep investing in these ideals by at least cultivating spaces for our little community to grow between the two of us.

But this day, Sarah was off at a writing seminar that my husband, Clay, had found for her—off for three weeks to adventures of her own with kindred spirits. How had she become my deepest-of-deep friend, whose soul mirrored my own, who had called to my hidden, inward parts to be excellent in my walk with God and to love Him in a worthy way? I could not have understood as a young mom how profoundly my children would become my "bestest" of friends, my confidants and spiritual companions. But now I see that this kind of relationship had to be planned, protected, fought for, scheduled into the busyness of real life. Close friendships come from significant investments of time and attention.

This is only part of our story. Our friendship grew through the natural storms and phases of childhood, the hormones of a tired mama, emotions shared, sharp words given and immediately regretted, finger-pointing attitudes that smoldered in our hearts as we walked through the normal pathways of mother and child.

We have had famous disagreements, tearful moments, misunderstandings, differing preferences and values, and hurt feelings. Yet part of the reason we are so very close is because we have learned to push through our inconsistencies, selfishness, and personality differences to grow towards health, bonding, and deep appreciation for the safe place our friendship and love have offered through the years of growth. Our commitment to always return to unconditional love and acceptance, to speak the words "I am sorry," to accept blame and humble ourselves, and to restore the relationship through the words "I am so grateful for you, and I love you so much. Will you please forgive me?" laid the foundation for trust deep inside our hearts for one another. We all need safe people we know will love us through every season. It is the foundation of mature relationships.

When my children were growing up, I had only a general notion about the long-term implications of intentionally investing in them. But now, as a woman in my mid-sixties, I understand better that often the first impressions of unconditional love, preferring one another, building close ties to each other's "beings" start in a mother-daughter or mother-son relationship. Though this is not a book about my sons, the principles we share in this book have cultivated the same results in their lives—we are all the closest of companions. As with my daughters, our close friendship has been wrought in the midst of personality differences, immature moments, times of fun, unconditional love, and the comfort of trusting each other with cherished dreams and secrets.

Mothers (and fathers) are often the ones who can give their children a strong foundation in relationships that will enable them to build deep and lasting friendships for their whole lives. If mothers learn to welcome their babies and nurse them with tender kisses; attach to them with touch, eyes of devotion, and love; give emotional affirmation; and focus on passing down a legacy of acceptance and cherishing, they are preparing their children to have strong, healthy friendships and love the rest of their lives. Mothers become the conduit for God's love to be felt through all stages of life. I think everyone needs a loving mama or a loving-mama figure their whole lives—someone who is committed to helping meet needs, no matter what. I still need a mama figure, even though my own mom passed away many years ago.

These foundations of health are dependent not only on mothers but on surrounding communities of people—mothers as well as fathers, grandparents, neighbors, pastors, teachers, peers. Our community has the potential to influence us in so many ways—whether by teaching us healthy habits for interacting with our surroundings or by modeling destructive behaviors.

Deep impressions or roadways are formed in the brain through countless experiences, and they are shaped by the small, daily events of relating to those around us. We come to adopt the habits of those who have formed us. Consequently, this area of relational skills influences the whole of our lives and is often shaped by the people surrounding us at the earliest ages—whether they're mature or immature, healthy or unhealthy. These patterns of relating influence our ability to feel good about ourselves, our ways of relating to others, our strength in marriage and our enjoyment of intimacy, and our ability to parent well. They also influence how we fit into our overall context in life.

Yet mothers, especially those who have not had healthy models of relationship, can pass on legacies of guilt, anger, manipulation, fear, critical attitudes, judgment, and insecurity, which give children holes in their emotional well-being—sometimes for their whole lives.

The profound role of mothers, uniquely ordained by God, has significant influence on generations of future adults. When mothers demonstrate that people can be a great source of security, dependability, and encouragement and provide roots and wings, then they can launch their children into the world ready to be competent in friendship, in marriage, and in the community. The children will have learned the pillars of how to establish healthy relationships in their first one, with their mama. This is expressed in the scientific research surrounding attachment theory.

I receive hundreds of letters each year from women who say that their backgrounds are so broken they don't even know where to begin. It can be overwhelming to see in ourselves anger, impatience, weariness, and failure in relationships—qualities that we feel will ruin our family in the long term. I kept wanting to have more children so I could "do it right" with at least one child.

But I have seen that God has taken my small basket of "fish and loaves" and made it enough to build the foundation for healthy community in spite of my failures. Be encouraged—He can restore health and beauty where we have brought darkness and scars. He loves to redeem relationships.

Friendship has deep significance for the entire fabric of our society. When connections are healthy, strong, and vibrant, then adults will live their lives with that strength. When this eminently important base of emotional health is not built on a string of virtuous relationships, bad habits of unhealthy relating and deep feelings of inadequacy and inferiority can grow in one's heart. Of course, no one has a perfect childhood, so most of us come to adulthood with a combination of good and bad relational habits. That's why it is so important that we correct unhealthy patterns of relating and replace bad experiences with healthy ones.

The idea of friendship did not just begin with us. God crafted into the very design of our hearts the ability to be known, to long for belonging to a community, and to celebrate life in the context of loving relationships—basically to be fulfilled by friendship. Family was one of the communities God created where friendship was intended to flourish. Yet the community of others—friends found through the pathways of life—is another one of the ways God intended for us to enjoy and share life so that we would not feel alone and isolated.

How thankful I am that God was the One who was seeking companionship when he put Adam and Eve in the Garden, where He walked among them (Genesis 3:8). Scripture tells of Moses speaking with God face-to-face, as one speaks to a friend (Exodus 33:11). Abraham was called the friend of God (James 2:23). We know the story of Jonathan and David, who had a famous friendship and lived to support and encourage one another (1 Samuel 18:3). Jesus lived with and loved and ate with His disciples as part of His philosophy of ministry, and He shared deeply in the sadnesses and celebrations of life with them. He pronounced, "You are my friends" (John 15:15). Friendship is literally written throughout the pages of Scripture. Our God didn't just impose a set of theological thoughts upon our minds, but He was the original friend—One who would understand our need for the kind of intimacy that would satisfy our souls.

God is the One who came up with the excellent idea of friendship. He is committed to it, He cultivates it in relationship with us, and He wants us to celebrate it and enjoy it our whole lives. Love through healthy relationships is the oxygen that fuels strong hearts, minds, and spirits.

The Challenge of Cultivating Friendship in a Broken World

Unfortunately, we do not always experience the richness and beauty God intended when He designed friendship. Brokenness entered the realm of friendships when the world fell.

Sitting in the soft, cool breezes coming off the ocean, my friend and I sat under an awning of a tiny café that bordered the sandy beach. With her back to anyone who would enter the coffee shop, she was trying to control the sobs that involuntarily overwhelmed her whole being, having been stored up her whole life. This is what she shared with me that day:

I have never told anyone my whole story. I was ashamed.
I thought it must have been my fault that my mother left
us when I was just seven years old. My mother was tired
of the responsibility of taking care of my siblings and me.
All through my childhood, I tried to ignore the feelings
that surged when others had their moms at school events,
when Mother's Day came and I didn't know where mine
was, when I entered my teen years and didn't have anyone
to talk to about my curiosity about my body and sex.
I look back now and realize I was suffocating with a need
to be loved and embraced for who I was by a mother who
would never be able to give that to me.

Eventually I looked for love in all the wrong places,
trying to fill the hole I felt from my mom's rejection.
But I also found that because I had grown up without
the experience of living with a mother I could trust,
I had a hard time trusting myself to other women. I felt
that they were unreliable. It has just been in recent years
that I understood I would need lots of counseling to
heal, to become whole, and that I was actually capable
of enjoying the delight of friendship with other women.

My friend went on to tell me that it had been a long road of
healing and that she had been in formal counseling for the past
eight years. I mostly just listened as she shared with me. My heart
broke for her as I heard about the wounds that cut so deeply
inside her. I realized that she had kept most of this covered up as
she pushed through life with a smile on her face. Gratefulness and
compassion filled my heart as I understood she had shared the
inner part of her soul. I wanted to be worthy of that trust.

This story my friend shared was reflective of the experiences of many precious women I have met with over the years. From the very beginning, God intended for us to know love, intimacy, and the pleasure of friendship. Yet one of the consequences of living in a world that is in rebellion against God's perfect plans is that many of us have grown up with a less-than-perfect home life and have not developed pathways in our brains for what healthy relationships look like.

Before we can truly enjoy the deep pleasure of girlfriends, we have to become healthy in our own lives. Learning to believe that we have great value, that God designed us well, and that we are precious to Him and to others is essential if we are to go into a friendship with a heart willing to give and to receive.

Professional counseling helped my sweet friend heal from the rejections and scars of her early life. All of us come with baggage of some kind, because none of us come from perfect backgrounds, not to mention that all of us are limited and self-centered. Having the wisdom and understanding of a trusted counselor or mentor is a way many of us can move from being victims to becoming gifts to those we meet.

When we seek healing for the wounds from earlier events in our lives, learn to humbly admit our faults, ask for forgiveness and healing for poor decisions, and embrace the boundless love God has for us, we become a resource of that wisdom and understanding for others. We often develop compassion and sympathy when we work through our own issues. Then, out of gratefulness, become an encouragement to others who are struggling with the same things we battled.

Most women long for someone who is real, who can accept them with all their flaws. Consequently, it is not our accomplishments and awards, not the ways we impress people, that cause them to want to be close to us. It is the feeling that we can be known and still loved that makes us feel safe with one another. We long for sympathy and understanding from someone who has walked a similar road to the one we have walked.

Let True, Biblical, Unconditional Love Build the Foundation of Friendship

A nurturing friendship begins with learning the ways of love. When we start to practice the behavior and actions of love, we open the door into a sound, close relationship.

Colossians 3:14 says, "Above all, clothe yourselves with love, which binds us all together in perfect harmony." I love this verse because it shows us a picture of what it looks like to love others. When we dress for the day, we cover our bodies from head to toe with clothes appropriate for the weather. We may put on a shirt and jeans, then a jacket, and finally socks and boots if it is a snowy winter's day.

Similarly, when we clothe ourselves in love, we cover ourselves—our hearts, minds, and souls—with the kind of love Jesus gave us, taking into account the people we will see and the needs they might have. It is acting through love that brings harmony, a blending of two different people into a unified relationship.

Learning the Ways of Love

Based on my experiences in friendship over the years, here are some of the steps I've discovered about learning to live in love.

1. LOVE YOUR NEIGHBOR AS YOURSELF.

Love in any relationship begins with being concerned about the needs of others, not just our own. We ponder how the other person is doing, what her needs are, how we might be an encouragement. We look for clues as to what is going on in her heart, since external behavior often masks the real feelings bubbling inside.

Loving others is expressed through many actions. Speaking words of affirmation and encouragement gives life. When we are serving others by being thoughtful, helping when someone has needs she can't meet herself, and initiating meeting together, we create an environment where memories are made and growing intimacy is shaped. Clothing ourselves in love means we seek to allow what we say, do, think, and express through our actions to be consistent with unconditional love.

We all hope that someone will show interest in us by asking us questions and seeking to find out what is on our hearts. But this is the art of communication. Learning to ask simple questions of our friends helps them to feel noticed. How many times have we been in gatherings where no one approaches us or asks us questions about ourselves? To be a friend, we must show ourselves friendly.

Years ago, I was at a conference for five days by myself and didn't know a single person. On the last day, a woman came up to me and said, "May I sit with you for lunch? Tell me about yourself. I would love to know your story." We ended up talking for two hours and missed the next session of our conference! But now, she is one of my dearest friends. This friendship came about because she showed interest in me—and still does.

2. EXHIBIT WISDOM, BOUNDARIES, AND LOYALTY.
Having worked in ministry for forty-plus years has meant that I have experienced every variety of relationship with other women. In some cases this has opened up blessings and wonderful connections, but unfortunately it has also led to interactions with people

who have unhealthy ways of engaging. At some point separation from an unhealthy person becomes necessary. Gossiping, controlling, lying, accusing, criticizing extensively, spreading rumors, being overly emotional, or being emotionally unresponsive are hindrances to developing sound relationships.

We all occasionally find ourselves in places where we must learn to set boundaries with people in order to function in a healthy way. A relationship that exhibits negative cycles over and over again, resulting in conflict and damage because of unhealthy responses, is one that requires us to draw lines of protection for ourselves. Every normal relationship goes through ups and downs. Yet when the factors that define a friendship include constant friction and discord, sometimes we are forced to take a step of separation from such a friend.

I used to think that being a mature Christian meant I needed to stay in all relationships, no matter the cost. Yet through experience, studying Scripture, and getting counsel, I have learned that some relationships must be terminated if I am to remain strong, emotionally healthy, and vibrant. We are always called to love, as "a friend loves at all times" (Proverbs 17:17, NASB), and Jesus commanded us to "love each other" (John 13:34). We are always called to forgive (Ephesians 4:32).

Yet Proverbs is full of admonitions about not engaging with fools. A fool is someone who is limited in wisdom and scorns understanding and truth. Reading Proverbs has helped me gain much insight into what the Bible has to say about relating to others. I can extend love, grace, and forgiveness to others from my heart, while knowing that I may not be able to relate to them on a personal level.

We should never be quick to break a relationship, and we

should do so only with the wise counsel of others, when our own assessment is confirmed by other mature people. But there are times when the wisest, most godly course of action is to continue to show love while not inviting the person into your inner circle. In my own life, these seasons of broken friendships have created heartbreak and sorrow. Through these times of brokenness, I have experienced loneliness and feelings of failure and have been open to self-condemnation.

But also through these times, I have found that there are friends who are loyal, supportive, loving, and generous with their actions and words, and they have helped bring healing and restoration to my own soul. Finding—and being—such a loyal friend is worth a treasure chest of jewels. My loyal, inner-circle friends have, through kindness, thoughtfulness, prayer, and walking with me on my journey, made it possible to find my footing, to heal, to move forward after hurt and rejection. I have also looked to the model of Christ to guide my own attitude. He did not seek to defend Himself but lived in the knowledge of God's justice and His friends' trust.

3. FORGIVE AND ALLOW YOURSELF TO BE FORGIVEN.

Understand that every person you become friends with is going to disappoint you at some point. No one is perfect, and that includes you. What we all long for is the grace that covers our blunders as well as someone who chooses to assume the best about us when we fail to be mature. So many times I have been an imperfect friend to my friends and my children. I intend to be patient, kind, and generous with them because I want them to know how much I love them, but sometimes I still blow it.

Not long ago, I began the morning with a desire in my heart to create a really special day and a great memory with our family. The Christmas holidays had come to an end, and two of my children were getting ready to go back to Scotland for school. I started out well.

I brought Joy a cup of tea while she was still in bed, lit candles for her, and put on some soft music. Desiring to surprise everyone with a great feast of a breakfast, I scurried to the kitchen to make four loaves of homemade whole-wheat bread.

When it was time to make breakfast, I moved into my Martha mode. I got irritated that I was the only one working while everyone else stumbled slowly into the kitchen. Before I knew it, I'd had a small explosion. I threw a wet blanket over the moods of everyone, and my good intentions were spoiled by my failure to control my spirit. I felt terrible, hating that I was leaving this bad memory in my children's minds as they left home.

After a very quiet breakfast, where everyone was trying to pretend my little outburst was not affecting them, I went upstairs to my bedroom to dwell on my own sense of failure.

An almost imperceptible knock came from my door.

"Come in?" I said, wondering if I had really heard a noise. Joy came in with a little tray, a lit candle, and a fresh cup of steaming tea in my favorite china cup.

"Mama, I have been thinking of all the ways you served us over Christmas. You are truly the best mama a girl could have. You delight me in so many ways. I wanted you to know that I am grateful for you. I know you must be tired from working so hard, and I wanted you to have a few moments by yourself breathing in peace. But I also wanted you to know no one is mad at you for your outburst. We love you so much."

Grace for the moment—that is what I needed. Her love covered over my sin and didn't even register it, just as 1 Peter 4:8 says: "Most important of all, continue to show deep love for each other, for love covers a multitude of sins." A friend covers her friend's shortcomings with love.

But the second part of covering sin with love is understanding that we must also forgive ourselves when we blow it. Part of this means we must give up the idea that we could have ever been perfect anyway! Living in constant guilt destroys our hearts. Once we blow it, we need to come to Christ and talk to Him about it: "God, I feel so bad that I got angry. I am so sorry. I know you forgive me. Will you please help me to restore my love and relationship with you so I can find peace? Help me to restore my relationship with my children, too. Please give me the grace to be more patient."

Only when we restore ourselves to God's heart and love are we able to restore our relationship with the one we have offended. By giving ourselves personal forgiveness, which comes from God, we can reach out and say "I'm sorry" to the one who has felt separated from us by our offense. When I have gone through the vulnerable process of offense, forgiveness, and restoration with my closest friends, it has actually given more worth to that relationship. Relationships build in value over years of time invested, one day at a time. There is a unique preciousness when two women have moved through challenges to unconditional love. This kind of friend is safe for us, and we can trust her with our whole heart because she has proved trustworthy. Sympathy and understanding create pathways to our inner hearts.

Knowing that there are people who have stood with us through every season, who have helped us stay strong, who have believed the best, and who have borne adversity with us means the world to us. In their love, we have found such grace and comfort. And we have discovered that when we wait, God is the generous justifier of our lives.

Even as I missed Sarah that day as I walked, I was thankful that I had such a precious friendship with her that was so worthy of missing. Friendship has become one of the works of my life—and one of the most satisfying ones, at that.

So much could be written about friendship, and our hope is that this book will inspire you to seek out more meaningful friendships or to build on the ones you have. No matter where you're starting from, meaningful companionship is built on these foundations: becoming a lover of people for the rest of your life; becoming healthy in your own emotional life so that you can give grace; determining to practice loving others in words, deeds, and joy; committing to be loyal to your friends through thick and thin; and deciding to serve those who you have called your friends. I feel even closer to my friends and my girls who have walked with me through my weaknesses and inconsistencies and still love and accept me. When we extend this kind of grace, forgiveness, and loyalty, we can be part of God's beautiful, redemptive work as He uses these friendships to heal one another's wounds.

CHAPTER 5

Saturday Mornings:
The Girls' Club Prototype

*True friendship is a very helpful thing indeed . . .
and we should have a very high ideal of it, and never
sully it by any failure in truth and sincerity. I fear
the name of friendship is often degraded to a kind of
intimacy that has nothing of real friendship in it.*

L. M. MONTGOMERY

SARAH ⁊ Saturday mornings are sacred times in Clarkson-girl economy. They mean good coffee, croissants, and the kind of conversation that sets you on your feet, excavates your heart, and readies you to dream. Wherever Clarkson girls are gathered in the world on a Saturday, be it in autumnal Oxford, in windy St. Andrews, or under the sapphire skies and snowy peaks of Colorado, there's bound to be a Girls' Club outing early in the morning.

We have kept this sacred time with each other since I was a teenager and my mom first whisked me away from the house early one Saturday morning to let me spill my angsty soul to her over a cup of coffee. Those mornings were my first model for what the friendship of women could look like in all its intelligence, courage, and laughing beauty. When I think about what it takes to cultivate friendship, a series of three Saturday memories comes to mind, each embodying a core value of Girls' Club friendship.

Friendship Means Being Intentionally and Deeply Known

The Colorado sun was already up, with strong golden light pouring through my window at the early morning hour when my mom shook me awake and put a finger to her lips.

"Shh, let's sneak out and get some breakfast," she said.

Sleepy teenager though I was, I came instantly awake at this chance to get my mother all to myself, and I quickly slipped on a sweater and jeans against the early morning mountain cold. We met downstairs, making it out the door and into the car without even disturbing the golden retriever. We zoomed into the wide morning, the rising sun on our faces, the quiet of the car expanding around us. I remember the relief of that quiet, the invitation it was to me as a teenager deeply struggling with my doubt of God, needing to talk but not sure how to, feeling that finally there was space just for me. I remember how I began to relax as we drove and chatted, how the deep things in my heart began to rise to the surface in the light of my mom's gentle questions.

We reached our favorite downtown French café, with its high ceilings and strains of Vivaldi, and settled at our usual table in the window. (We felt very proprietary about that table—how dare anyone else sit there?) We gripped mugs of strong coffee and nibbled at our shared egg-and-bacon (crispy, please!) croissant. And when my stomach was full and my muscles a little more relaxed, my mom turned her eyes full to mine, leaned in, and asked me what was going on in my heart.

"What's bothering you?" she said. I knew that whatever it was, she would listen. "How is your soul?"

To this day, it's a question we girls ask each other on Saturday-morning talks and long phone calls, a question that embodies one of the first gifts that came to me through the Girls' Club: to be intentionally and deeply known. One of the first things I learned about friendship from those mornings was the way close relationships are nourished by people who ask intentional questions, who make space for other people to speak out what is deepest and most urgent in their hearts. As a daughter, I knew that our Saturday mornings were my chance to tell Mom all that was going on in my heart, to let my introverted self speak out the thoughts that crowded in my head. This was my space to complain or cry, to admit to loneliness or try out a new idea or articulate a new dream.

Those first conversations created a pattern for cultivating relationships that helped me, in turn, ask probing, gentle questions of my mom as I grew into an adult. Those mornings taught me to understand friendship as a space in which we as women learned to see each other well, to help each other be known. They taught me to bring attention and purpose to the space of friendship so that our conversations became a place in which I learned how to articulate what was in my heart, to know myself well, and to begin to know someone else.

Those patterns of intentionality and depth shape my friendships to this day. In a busy world where conversation often skims only the surface events of our lives, it is a powerful gift to create the space and atmosphere in which another woman, a friend, has the chance to share what is most urgently real in her heart. It's a unique gift I can bring to new friendships, a kind of relational hospitality that invites a new girlfriend to not just chat about the surface stuff but to foray into the deeper realms of hope and prayer, ideals and dreams. In knowing and sharing those sacred spaces, friendship finds its roots and energy. We women give each other the gift of intentionality by making the space and asking the questions—skills I first learned on early Saturday mornings over cups of strong coffee. Is it any wonder I'm convinced that cups of strong coffee go hand in hand with all good things?

Friendship Means Pursuing Excellence

Booted, be-coated, and wrapped to our chins in scarves, Joy and I crept out the big front door of our college and into the damp October air. Up the sidewalks we scuffed in the early morning hush, the autumn trees afire over our heads, the wind sending leaves like sparks through the air as we shivered in the cold and made a run for the coffee shop just up the road, where the current Girls' Club Saturday mornings were kept.

We were both in Oxford for studies of various kinds, and these were our weekly, sisterly trysts for catch-up and coffee. We settled onto the (woefully uncomfortable) wooden bench seats, put our hands around the blue patterned cups brimming with delicious flat whites, split our almond croissant, and began to talk a thousand miles an hour.

It was a season of rich learning for both of us, and in those swift, glorious talks, we reveled in the joy of discovery, the sense of new space and capacity filling up our souls. I was afire with my study of the Incarnation, the way Christ's taking on flesh made every corner of Creation a space that redemption could reach so that even ordinary life—home and hearth, cooking and art, story and feast—became a place where God's Kingdom could come. Joy was alight with what she'd been studying about virtue, the way beauty draws us to love what is good and music teaches us to hunger for truth. One insight led to another; her point on music reminded me of something I'd read on prayer. We told each other books to read and poems to check out, music to discover and favorite lectures to explore. When we finally took a breath, the silence between us crackled with the golden energy that comes when two people kindle delight and curiosity in each other. "Iron sharpens iron" (Proverbs 27:17) had never felt so true.

The energy and fun of that Oxford moment, the joy we took in sharing what we had learned, symbolizes an aspect of the Girls' Club that is fundamental to our concept of friendship: the love of learning and the pursuit of excellence. Those Oxford mornings were precious in the story of Joy's and my sisterly friendship, but sharing what we had learned in both mind and spirit was something we had long practiced on other Girls' Club mornings. My parents raised us all to be readers, and as far back as I can remember, my mom asked me to tell her about what book I was currently loving—whether that was a tome on the Inklings' theories of imagination or a slim volume of poetry by Seamus Heaney or my latest favorite novel by George Eliot.

But far before that, I remember watching my mom at her own reading. As a little girl, I learned her pattern of having a devotional book or a novel always on hand. I recall stealing the Philip Yancey books she kept in a stack by her Bible, loving what they taught me about grace. To this day, I know that my mom will always be learning (I recently stole her copy of Henri Nouwen's collected letters), ready to tell me how her mind has stretched since we last talked. I know the same is true for Joy, whose vim to understand ethics and music, whose capacity to debate the big questions of culture and faith, always leaves me hungry to learn far more than I already do.

The Girls' Club taught me that I, as a woman, was made to think, to learn, to question, to read, to grow. The habits of reading and deep thought are central to my concept of womanhood, my idea of friendship—realities I have encountered in my most beloved mentors and companions. The women I am closest to are those who have the identity of learners, made by God to think, to be rich in wisdom, and to use that wisdom to create, lead, inspire, and give. One of the great delights of my adult life, rooted in those Saturday mornings, has been the joy of knowing strong, curious, spiritual women. What my mom modeled and what Joy and I both cultivated as we matured was a companionship based on shared ideals and convictions. We understood each other as created for meaning and depth, and one of the functions of our Saturday-morning friendship was to challenge and spur each other to growth—in spiritual commitment, in the life of learning, in our quest for ideals and beauty.

When we girls gather together these days, we know we'll learn from each other. Joy's thesis on virtue and art drives me to yearn for excellence in my own life, to create stories that will sate that hunger in others. My mom's writing on discipleship and relationship calls me constantly back to that core relationship I am made to cultivate with Christ. Their passion for what they are learning convicts me, kindles me to fresh life, reminds me of the joy and gift of what it means to be a woman who thinks and reads, who reaches for excellence in all she does. Our friendship is a space of refreshment that we visit when we are weary, a place where we call one another back to excellence ourselves.

And oh, the delight of intelligent women ready to change the world together. There's nothing like it.

Friendship Means Celebrating Beauty and Pursuing Dreams

"Oh look," said my mom, hooking her arms through Joy's and mine. "It's a symphony in the sky. Ah, doesn't it just make you want to create something beautiful?"

The morning sky over Mount Hermon, our favorite craggy old foothill, was crimson and rose and gold. The clouds whirled like ocean waves, the new light soaking the mountain fields and slopes and the tops of the rugged firs in gold. We three stood together, breathing the cool air, our eyes opened to the grandeur of God charging the world (as Gerard Manley Hopkins so beautifully wrote). I was back in Colorado for a springtime visit, and after our usual outing for coffee and conversation and a cheesy egg quesadilla (our current favorite), we went for a long walk, the last of the central rhythms that form a Girls' Club Saturday morning. We often walk the streets of an old Colorado neighborhood, where friendly old houses peek out from behind ancient trees. But the beauty of the springtime world took us into the mountains that day. Together we watched and wondered.

My mom's expression of delight drew us into a space of attention in which we noticed the glory of the world together. That's something we've done together for as long as I can remember. I've walked with my mom and sister in countless places over the years, and those walks are always marked by the time we take to notice the beauty of the world, letting the loveliness of creation grow in us, shaping our hopes and desires. We've walked in every state we've lived in—on old Texas trails, down forested Tennessee roads amid mosquitoes and heat, up the red-rock trails of Colorado. We've walked in Asheville, past big gardens and gracious old houses that made us dream of big families and long-term homes. We've strolled up the Prince Edward Island beaches on our long-awaited visit to "Anne's land," where we three girls sat on the sand dunes under a summer moon and told each other everything we hoped to create and reach for in the future. Those walks, so crammed with loveliness, helped me discover another aspect of the Girls' Club friendship that is core to our identity: the celebration of beauty and the pursuit of dreams.

One of the gifts I love most in my friendship with my girls is that we help each other to experience the fullness of God's presence and goodness. For us, that means a real celebration of what He has given in Creation—not just in the outdoor glory we find in our walks, but in the ordinary grace of good food and lovely moments, of music and good books, of feasts and coffee. We savor the deliciousness of life together in those excellent coffees and croissants; notice the drama of the seasons, the way the whole of human existence is crammed with small beauties that wait for our attention.

But hand in hand with that will to see God's beauty is a fierce belief that He gives us dreams and that He calls us to follow Him into new creativity, adventures, and challenges. We wonder together at the story He is weaving in our own lives.

The habit of celebrating beauty has often led us into wondering exactly how we are called to create and bring it into the world. Girls' Club mornings, especially during those long, wondering walks, are the space in which we girls dream together. As we marvel at the scope of God's goodness, it quickens us together to hope, to imagine, to dream of what might just be possible.

What do you hope for? What are your ideals? What do you think God is calling you to become? Those questions, and the long walks in which we untangled them, are deeply formative, marked by a shared commitment to the open horizons of possibility made real by faith. I often felt that walking was our way of reaching in vision towards the ideals that most drove us, the dreams of study or artistry, travel or ministry that filled our hearts. Many of the dreams I spent years pursuing—books and Oxford study, marriage, home—were spoken first in those lovely hours of deep friendship on those long, wondering walks.

How Does a Girls' Club Happen?

There you have the Girls' Club prototype. I was an adult, out in the world and figuring out my own patterns of friendship, before I realized how deeply the Saturday morning prototype had shaped me. When I reflect on what is central to the cultivation of friendship, I think back to those three fundamental values—those core ideas that drive the way my mom and sister and I have always related and grown together. Those values had to be chosen, pursued, and maintained with diligence over many years, and as I consider what it takes to cultivate them in friendship, I realize that those Saturday mornings taught me something else as well.

Deep, long-term, soul-satisfying friendship takes hard work.

Companionship of soul and mind requires planning, purpose, and choice. Those treasured Saturday spaces, and the community that grew from them, didn't just happen on their own. Saturday mornings were chosen and claimed times, times when we said no to other invitations or work. My mom chose to spend time with her young daughters over the lure of work or sleep, or just an hour of relaxation by herself. Joy and I now choose those times together and with dear local friends over countless other social and academic commitments in our own lives. When we are together, our conversations continue to be shaped by thoughtful questions purposefully asked, by our intent to know and be known. This is why the Girls' Club camaraderie has lasted through many years, even though the three of us have at times lived thousands of miles apart.

Friendship isn't something that just happens, a gift dropped into our laps to be received. Friendship, I have come to understand, is something we both create and give, a work and an art we make space for again and again, a priority we choose amid the demands of life. Friendship requires concerted, often intensive effort—something I have often had to remind myself of when starting again in a new place. As an idealistic, introverted, and often lonely twenty-something, I think I often sat around waiting for friendship to happen. I was confused as to why the magical invitation—to friendship, to love, to community—didn't fall into my lap. I wondered if I was in the wrong place or wrong church, and if friendship would happen if I just moved somewhere else. I had what Wendell Berry calls in his short story "Pray without Ceasing" the "characteristic disease" of the modern age—the assumption that I would be better off or a better person in a different place.

What I came to understand was that the power to invite lay with me. Just as my mom drew her girls into regular times of relationship, I, too, could create the space and time in which friendship could take place. One of the most empowering things you can come to understand about relationships is that you are always an agent; as a woman made in the image of God, you have the power of love always at your fingertips. No matter how insecure or inadequate you feel, no matter how lonely you have been, the truth about your identity is that you are always powerful in the capacity to initiate; to love; to offer yourself; to create the time, space, and intention in which relationships can happen and friendships begin.

As Rowan Williams observes in his book *Dostoevsky: Language, Faith, and Fiction* regarding Dostoevsky's remarkable characters, each person alive has the power to be an incarnational presence, a person in whom the horizons of new possibility are opened simply by the choice to love. One of the first areas of doctrine I studied at Oxford made this powerfully clear to me. In an early paper on the Incarnation, I encountered the reality that when Christ took human flesh and came into the world, He started the story of humanity all over again. He scratched out the ending words of sin and death and began to write a new chapter by His loving, holy presence. Just as God spoke Creation into being from nothing at the beginning of time, Jesus spoke new life, love, and redemption into being out of the darkness of death. The amazing thing is that any person who follows Christ, any woman who walks by the power of the Holy Spirit, is filled with the same creative, story-starting power that drove the creation and redemption of the universe. With Christ in you, you can look into the emptiness, or even the darkness of loneliness, and speak love, friendship, and possibility into being.

You do this by your use of time and space, the daily gift of possibility that God gives to us and we give to each other when we shape them by our will to love. In Genesis, at the dawn of human existence, God spoke the Creation mandate (Genesis 1:28), giving shape to what it means to be human by commanding the people He had created to bring order to the new world, to fill it with life and love, to continue the cultivation of the earth and the cultivation of relationships that He began when He made such a beautiful and good world. To cultivate friendship in the midst of a fallen existence, to fill loneliness with relationship, is part of that ongoing, fundamental work, renewed and enriched by the love of Christ filling our hearts, reaching out to others through us.

But how is this work begun? What does it look like to be a creator of friendship? What does love look like in action? These questions were answered for me by my mom's model of Girls' Club cultivation, the answers I remembered when I gathered up my courage and stepped out of my twenty-something introversion to create friendship myself. And these are the answers I want to explore in the rest of this chapter, expanded by the great friends I have encountered whose wisdom and creativity added to the pattern I first received in the Girls' Club. Those answers can be described by five progressive actions that I think are central to the powerful cultivation of friendship in the life of any woman: invite, plan, provide, stay, and pray.

Invite

The first day I moved into my dorm room at Oxford, I met Alice, another student who lived just down the hallway. In those early days of my new life in England, blurred by jet lag and all the swift adjustments required by a new culture and a rigorous student schedule, I barely had margin for sleep, let alone for new friendships. But Alice was a constant presence, a gracious companion who drew me out of the isolation of being new to everything by her continued habit of inviting me to things: to a punting trip (a very English occupation that basically means sailing down the river in a boat propelled by a long pole), for a snack in her room, for a first visit to chapel. I blindly accepted, more from exhaustion than real engagement, but soon I came to look forward to Alice's knock on the door. It always meant something delightful—a snack, a joke, a walk in the park, a chat in her room.

Those first invitations soon opened the door to a whole year of delightful and rich friendship, one marked by late-night talks with bits of chocolate, by Oxford adventures, and by shared theological wrestlings that soon included a third friend, Ali, and made us a kindred trio. We three became bosom friends, and I marvel at the depth our friendship reached in the brief academic year we shared. Three years later, we are still close, a fact I am convinced was made possible by Alice's loving choice to invite those around her into the space of friendship. I saw her gift for initiating again when we three friends dispersed to (literally) the far corners of the earth, and Alice created a group for us on a shared messaging app so we could keep up with each other. Her initiation creates space for friendship and loyalty to grow. She is a radiant example of what I think is one of the first actions of real friendship: *invitation*.

There's an almost enchanted power when one person invites another to share, whether it's a cup of tea, a conversation, an autumn walk, or a meal. The words open up a new realm of possibility. "Come to my house for a chat" is a little like "Once upon a time"—words that signal the advent of a whole new story, a fresh realm of relational possibility. The power to invite, to create the specific time and space for friendship and ask another person into it, lies in every one of us. You and I have this power available to us every single day, a huge force of possibility that we can choose to use for creativity and relationship.

Integral to that power of invitation, though, is our willingness to offer ourselves to another, to see ourselves as givers. It requires that we take on the identity of someone not only waiting to receive friendship but to give it, to start it, to offer our time and home as a gift to others. I saw this throughout my childhood in the way my mom opened our home for tea parties, Bible studies, and family meals. We moved about a dozen times by the time I was eighteen, and loneliness was something we often felt as we started to create and find community again. But in each new place I watched as, once more, my mom invited a few new friends for a meal, kept up our tradition of a mother-daughter Christmas tea, or invited a few women to read some Scripture or an interesting book and discuss it once a week. I learned early in my life that friendship wasn't something we sat and waited for in our new home; it was something we created within it, a gift we gave to others by the choice of invitation.

Plan

One summer in my mid-twenties, I found myself at home with no plans. Summer can be a strange time in the life of a twenty-something, suspended between studies or seasonal work, with all the usual activities of church or community suddenly on hold. That year, I found myself in danger of the loneliness and boredom that come with such a season. But I was rescued by my good friend Ruth and her brilliant idea. Ruth was an old friend who was also back in town for the summer, also wondering what to do with the extra time, and she had come up with a plan to keep both of us enjoying life to the full.

Her plan was for us to meet weekly for a friendly meal at one of the many ethnic restaurants tucked into the older parts of Colorado Springs. We could explore world cuisine while discussing books and generally enjoying life together. How could I refuse such an intriguing and delightful invitation? Thus began a rich season of our friendship as we tried all sorts of new food—Ethiopian in Old Town, Mexican at the family-owned restaurant by the river, French at an old café, Moroccan at a sprawling old restaurant in the hills. We talked for hours, savoring our meals, trying new dishes, exchanging notes on the books we were reading over the summer—my current fascination with the English writer Elizabeth Goudge, Ruth urging me to attempt a bit of David Foster Wallace. Every week I looked forward to our next meal as the open summer days took shape with our shared adventures.

Ruth and her brilliant idea are a beautiful example of what it means to plan for friendship. Ruth didn't just suggest we get together now and then, leaving it to chance whether and how it would happen. Rather, she considered what we would both enjoy, what would keep us meeting regularly, and what would enrich our conversation and friendship. Her thoughtful planning created the space for our friendship to be regular and deep, centered on shared experience, marked by good conversation and exploration. Good things—like friendship, a happy home, beautiful memories—rarely just happen. They are planned and worked for, and the people who have them have chosen the good work of preparation—a work that doesn't require anything more than considering *when* you will make space for friendship, *how* you will fill that time, and *who* you want to spend it with.

The habit of planning isn't just a personality trait; it's a skill—a skill you can hone and grow, one common to great leaders, artists, teachers, heroes . . . and great friends. Planning is a habit we see modeled in Scripture in figures such as Lady Wisdom, who prepared her table and made a feast for those she invited into her home (Proverbs 9:1-2). Or Jesus, who invited His disciples to a hot breakfast (John 21:12) or drew them away to share a space of intensive teaching and prayer before His death (John 13–17). To plan for friendship is to create the world in which it happens. Invitation starts the story of a friendship; planning sets the scene, creating the world in which friendship will grow.

Provide

It's a delightful thing to inherit a friendship, something I richly received in my friendship with Gwen, one of my mom's oldest and dearest friends. Of all the women I know, Gwennie is a model of what I think is the third vital action of friendship: the choice to provide. To come to Gwennie's home is to come to a place that has been prepared for you—fresh sheets on the bed, a carefully chosen meal on the table, a lovingly selected gift, a book or quote or beauty she has saved to share.

When I was sixteen, I visited Gwennie for an early graduation trip to her home in Vienna. She met me at the airport with two huge bouquets of roses and took me home to a summery meal of chicken and Greek salad culled from the open-air markets. Over the requisite cup of Viennese coffee, she told me her grand plans for my stay. She had carefully planned for delights: a series of outdoor adventures in the Austrian lake district, coffee at the famed Sacher Hotel, a massage and manicure for my sixteenth birthday in a little town just over the Hungarian border. She had planned movies for us to watch each quiet night (this was where my love of Kenneth Branagh's *Much Ado about Nothing* began), new recipes to cook together, Scripture for us to ponder in the mornings. Her gift to me that summer wasn't just the space of her home; it was her careful provision of days shaped and filled by her love.

Phyllis, another old friend and dear mentor, says that when we prepare and provide for friends, it's a way of showing love. When a guest arrives to a table set with china, a homemade cake, or a quote or Scripture set out for encouragement, she knows that she is valued. Love speaks in what we have prepared for the friends we invite into our homes. I have spent years attending Bible studies at Phyllis's home, I've stayed at her home, and I've had countless one-on-one visits, and each time, I feel her love expressed through the teatime trays she prepares, the lovely rooms she invites me into, the Scripture she always has ready to share with me.

Preparation is one of the key ways in which we have the capacity to deepen our friendships, to root them in shared moments of beauty, of prayer, of thoughtful conversations. This can be done both by preparing a physical space—good food, good music, beauty to sate the soul—and by preparing mind and heart, by considering the questions that might take a conversation to deeper waters.

My friend Mari, whom I met in Oxford, has been a marvelous example to me of friendship and community made meaningful by her preparation. Having planned an evening discussion themed on a single word or concept (*silence* or *love*), she asked friends from very different walks of life to reflect on what that word meant in their own lives and particular work, and to come ready to share. By preparing that meeting, by planning and shaping it, she made the space for a remarkable time of community and growth.

A final aspect of provision that is crucial in our time is simply the provision of attention. To be fully present with someone—to clear away the distractions of our technology, our busyness, our entertainment, our worries—is a gift that has become increasingly rare. We as a modern people live in the presence of our phones, we have beeps and rings and buzzers at every turn, we have countless tasks to complete and deadlines to meet. To offer a friend the whole of our attention, the fullness of our gaze, is to offer her the gift of our full selves—something crucial to long-term friendship.

Stay

Having moved many times, I am deeply aware of the way friendships can be lost.

I am thus profoundly grateful for the friends who made it their business to stay in touch—the ones whose friendships were shaped by a commitment to faithfulness. Katrina is one of my oldest and best friends. We haven't lived in the same state (or at times, even the same country) since we were thirteen and fifteen. But over the twenty-something years of our friendship, we have remained close in heart and connected in spirit, and it is simply because we chose to cultivate what we already had, to be faithful to the friendship we had been given. When I was living in Oxford for the first time, years ago, I got a message from Katrina one cold, wintry evening that her passport was all ready.

"For what?" I asked.

"To visit you!" she replied.

And she did, within the next month, taking time off from her work and family to hop the Atlantic "pond" and spend time with me roaming the Lake District.

She did this, going to all the trouble of planning, because our friendship was dear to her, something she made space to cultivate even in the midst of her own busy life. That same friend has written me hundreds of letters over the years, as I have her; we've visited back and forth, we've taken weekend trips together, and we've shared books through the mail. She even sends me birthday packages in England (no small feat!). We'll probably never get to live in the same place, but we remain bosom friends to this day. We just keep on planning for how our friendship will continue.

One of the key actions of friendship is simply the decision to be faithful. This core element works on several different levels within a friendship, weaving it together into a long-term reality. The first key to staying is simply the commitment to keep seeking the other. To be faithful in loving, present and regular in reaching out. Second, and crucially, to stay is also to learn to forgive, to embrace the imperfect or irritating aspects of a friend as well as her loveliness. To stay is to endure past the first glow of easy, kindred-spirit companionship through all the years of difficulty or separation or sorrow.

I have been deeply shaped in recent years by the writing of Wendell Berry, and one of the concepts he has illumined for me is the idea of fidelity—the same word we use to describe faithfulness in marriage. Fidelity, says Berry, is one of the qualities missing from the modern world:

> What fidelity is meant to protect—is the possibility of moments when what we have chosen and what we desire are the same. Such a convergence obviously cannot be continuous. No relationship can continue very long at its highest emotional pitch. But fidelity prepares us for the return of these moments, which give us the highest joy we can know; that of union, communion, atonement (in the root sense of at-one-ment).[1]

In our hurry-up, multiple-option, online society, we can always leave someone or something we find difficult—a person, a place, a church, a friendship. There is always another option. But real community, long-term friendship, and marriage are precious gifts only to be kept by a commitment to remain in the circle of love they create. As Berry so eloquently states, fidelity helps us to remain and to return to the love we first knew, to kindle it afresh, over and over again. Fidelity is a gift we can choose to give within a fallen world.

As an introverted idealist, my impulse is to bolt from a relationship at the first whiff of discord or unpleasant difference. I can always find a reason a church or small group is just not quite my thing; it's far too easy for me to simply let silence grow in a friendship where a difference of opinion or a personality has kindled conflict. But I've learned over many years that I have to resist my impulse to forsake what I do have in search of something more perfect. To remain has been one of the disciplines I've had to learn time and again, but it has also become the space in which a fragile, precious grace has grown. I've learned that the kind of friendship, the love, I so crave grows *out of* conflict faced, faults forgiven, sadness shared. Those difficult seasons create the soil in which love can root. Faithfulness, grace, and forgiveness are the rains that fall on the soil bringing a relationship to fuller growth.

We in the Girls' Club have known countless conflicts, big and small. We've wrestled with personality issues, with family quirks, with discouragement, with depression. The love that has grown between us is rooted in years of hard, loving choice. Our friendship isn't perfect or even easy; it's a good thing won by the fact that each of us chooses to fight the good fight of love, winning our way back to each other when we come apart.

Pray

For many years now, I have used a lovely little book of Celtic prayers in my morning devotions, and one particular prayer has gently shaped the way I think about my friendships. The closing canticle of the morning liturgy opens with a request for Christ to invade every corner of one's experience:

Christ, as a light illumine and guide me
Christ, as a shield overshadow me.

And it's followed by this request:

[Christ] Be in the heart of each to whom I speak;
in the mouth of each who speaks unto me.[2]

When we are able to recognize that each person to whom we relate, each person with whom we seek to cultivate a friendship, is made in the image of God, revealing a facet of His beauty, our hearts are opened to that person in a profound way. All friendship begins with the fact of God's great love; it is the origin of every other love. And as we foray into friendship, as we seek to relate and create connection in a difficult world, we do it in company with Christ, powered by His Spirit to initiate, to remain, to provide, to give.

You are never alone in this great work of friendship; God is always first, loving you and filling you in such a way that you can reach out to others. This daily prayer helps me to remember that fact, to be present to the Love that has already initiated towards *me*. Those words waken me to how loved I am in such a way that love burgeons in me, spilling onto others. Sometimes it is the simple remembrance of that fact that sets me on my feet once more, girds me with the strength I need to reach out yet one more time.

I write this with a new little baby girl sleeping on my chest. She's the newest member of the Girls' Club, and already I have countless plans for the memories we will make, the friendship I so deeply hope we form. I pray daily that I will know how to reach out to her in loving relationship. I pray that I will have the strength to be an initiator even in busy or weary times, one who forms our hours as mother and daughter by my choice to fill the time with spaces of friendship and deep conversation, of beauty (and buttery croissants) shared, of walks taken. Already, I try to make time each day to listen to music with this little one, to talk to her about all the beauty around us, to share the wonder of the springtime glory invading our little corner of the world. But one of these days, in whatever city our adventures take us to, on a Saturday morning I'll wake her up early so we can sneak out into the quiet of the early city, eat our croissants, and talk the morning away.

CHAPTER 6

Dating Your Friends

You can't stay in your corner of the
Forest waiting for others to come to you.
You have to go to them sometimes.

INSPIRED BY A. A. MILNE

JOY  We met at the mailboxes.

The funny thing is, we had once stood not two feet apart from each other on an awards stage when we were in high school. We both competed in speech and debate, and Elena beat me, but I barely remember that because I was so happily stunned to have made it that far in my first year of competitive speech and debate. But there we stood, side by side, waiting to hear our names, to see which trophy we received. I remembered her name, but we did not meet—at least not then.

Of all the places in the country, Elena and I chose the same tiny, private school to attend for university. Uncharacteristically for her deeply introverted self, Elena friended me on Facebook and sent an earnest and eager message noting our speech and debate connection and soon-to-be shared university. Uncharacteristically for me, I accepted this friend request from a familiar-sounding stranger and responded with equal earnestness. The July before we went to college, we exchanged polite messages, expressing our excitement and perplexity at what this new world of university would be like. We were like tiny baby birds, peering over the edge of our comfortable nests at the great world below. We decided it would be nice to meet when we got to school.

Not knowing the campus, we agreed on the most central landmark we could think of: the mailboxes.

It was oppressively hot that day as I peered around, waiting for Elena. The heady humidity of that August day mixed with the scores of new faces and accumulating pile of orientation paperwork made me feel small and a bit dizzy. Elena rounded the corner with a dignified urgency in her step, saw me, smiled, and waved. I felt a warm wave of relief; in all this newness, there was a friendly face smiling at me. She was wearing a sea-green dress, a color with which I have associated her ever since. We made our way to the well-beloved but also oft-bewailed campus coffee shop, wittily called Common Grounds. As we sipped iced lattes, we fell into surprisingly easy conversation, punctuated by exclamations of our disorientation at the newness of everything. Later that evening, we sat next to each other at the welcome banquet. I asked her what her favorite movies and books were. We talked about *Anne of Green Gables*, *The Lord of the Rings*, and Christopher Nolan. Over the course of the dinner, we talked and laughed, and by the end declared one another kindred spirits.

Only three weeks later, we were debate partners (one of the

few girl/girl teams in the league), faithful study companions, and cohorts for most of the delights and absurdities of freshman year. Neither of us having a car, we often trekked together on foot to get groceries or to spend the afternoon at Panera Bread (the only café within walking distance), eating macaroni and cheese and doing homework. In the evenings we would lie on my dorm room floor, eat dark-chocolate almonds, stare at my fairy lights, and bit by bit, divulge our dreams and fears and hopes.

Today those times feel like a distant dream, but Elena is still my kindred spirit. Our friendship looks different now that we live on different continents, but our bond is too tight to be broken by airfares or time zones. We are no longer tethered to the same rhythms that college provided, and seeing each other is not as easy as popping down the hall, but the richness of our friendship makes the costliness of time together worth it. Together we braved the newness of university, and ever since we've been side by side (sometimes via Skype) braving the ambiguities of life after college, of good jobs and bad jobs, of heartbreaks and falling in love, of doubts and discoveries, of adventures and sleepy seasons of life. We've fought and made up, cried and celebrated, and eaten an unreasonable number of quesadillas. When I read a good book, I text her. When she watches a thoughtful episode of a TV show, she calls me. We pray for each other.

In one of my undergraduate communication courses, we studied W. K. Rawlins's six stages of friendship.[1] As I read them to Elena, she quipped that we must have skipped immediately from the first stage of acquaintance to whatever stage lying on a dorm-room floor eating dark-chocolate almonds might be. It seems there was something special and immediate about our friendship, almost magical.

As I write this, I'm keenly aware that nothing I might say in these pages could sufficiently honor the weightiness and delight of my friendship with Elena. Sometimes I am struck by the oddity of how it came about—was it just fate? In some ways, it does feel as though we were kindred spirits, just waiting to discover each other. But I don't think this is quite true. My friendship with Elena has lasted not simply because we were magically best pals but because we had a great deal in common, because the activities of our lives helped to bond us together, and because we both have committed to our friendship. Friendship is magical, but often its magic comes as a result of initiating, investing, and maintaining a close friendship. We should ask God to guide us to kindred spirits and to put people in our path, but we must also be faithful to pursue and cultivate the opportunities for friendships that God makes available to us.

We need friendship, but it is not easy. Friendship has always required cultivation, and I think this is all the more true in our frenetic, digitally connected, and relationally disconnected times. So if life-giving friendships will not drop from the sky into our laps, we must learn to diligently pursue and wisely cultivate these relationships. We need a strategy, a plan.

I recently saw a friendship app—like a dating app, but for finding friends. At first I was amused, but then I was struck by a thought: Shouldn't we be as intentional about finding good, lifelong friends as we are about finding a mate? I could fill my whole house with books about dating—how to go about finding, courting, and committing to a relationship with a romantic partner. Most people have (or should have) some philosophy when it comes to finding a romantic partner. When we think of dating someone, we think of a matrix of activities, approaches, tips, and steps of commitment. Whatever your take on dating (or whatever you wish to call it), everyone seems to share the general assumption that there are wise and unwise ways to pursue romantic relationships. I think we ought to invest as much effort in thinking about how to wisely pursue friendship.

We need to learn to be as intentional about choosing and cultivating life-giving friendships as we are about choosing a mate. This involves thinking carefully about the way we go about initiating friendships, what we look for in a friend, and how we move towards commitments with friends in a wise and healthy way.

In short: let's learn to date our friends.

Initiation: Going First in Friendship

I think we idealize friendship the way we idealize falling in love: someday the right person (our future best friend forever!) will come along, we will click, we will never disagree on anything, and it will fill in all the cracks in our heart. Just like that—just like magic. And it's true that sometimes there is an Anne and Diana kind of magnetism or a particular situation or season that bonds us close and fast with someone. But I am of the opinion that in friendship, as in romance, even the most magical of connections will wither and fade away without intentional cultivation. And often the best friendships are not the ones that fall into our laps but the ones we actively pursue.

We all long for close relationships, but more often than not, we languish in loneliness, wishing someone would come along, initiate a relationship, pursue us, understand us. And this is not unreasonable. But it is good to remember that we all want to be pursued in friendship. Isn't the most sensible thing, then, to be proactive? One of the most rewarding decisions I've made is to be an initiator.

Initiating simply means being willing to be the person who makes the first move. Be the house where people know they can come. Ask the person you always have those interesting conversations with at church to have coffee with you sometime. Invite the person you think might be a kindred spirit at work to go on a hike with you this weekend. Host a movie night, make popcorn, and take pride in being a fabulous hostess.

My friendship with Elena was made possible because she reached out first. I think becoming an initiator comes with a sort of identity shift: you begin to see yourself as a conductor of friendships, a generous host, a conduit for togetherness. Beginning to see yourself this way becomes an incredibly rewarding part of your identity, and it moves you from a place of passive longing to active pursuit of friendships.

Initiation applies not only to activity but also to intimacy. One of the simplest and most profound ways to do this is through asking good questions.

In the first weeks of my master's program at St. Andrews, I met what felt like a million people. By the end of the first weekend of tumbling from orientation to introduction barbecue to evening gatherings, I had a hundred names and faces swimming around in my brain. After all these events, I began to perfect what I fondly referred to as the elevator pitch for my life: my name, what I was studying, where I was from, what degree program I was in, what I planned on doing with my degree. It was like an email autoresponder, but with human beings holding precarious plates of unappetizing snacks. I would leave these events feeling utterly exhausted and, ironically, quite unknown.

One evening in the first week, I found myself conveniently situated near the food and drink table. Through a session of inner squabble, I had convinced myself that it would be good to attend this event. But as I braced myself for another "professional" interaction, I started to wonder if I wasn't as extroverted as I thought I was. Out of the coiffed crowd, a bright-faced woman with curly blonde hair made her way over to me. She introduced herself, and I prepared for the elevator pitch.

"What program are you in?" she asked.

"Theology," I said a little bashfully. There is nothing that will shut down a conversation at a secular university like saying you study theology. "Theology and the arts, actually."

"Oh! How interesting!" she said with a sparkle in her eye. "It sounds like there's a story behind that. How did you come to study that?"

I was disarmed and delighted. Suddenly I was no longer a living, breathing résumé but a person with a story. I felt seen, deemed interesting. Her good question opened a causeway to closeness.

My St. Andrews friend knew one of the great secrets of forging a friendship: the surpassing value of a good question.

I like to think each one of us is like a house with many rooms. There's the front hall—it's pretty small, but it's where we invite most people, where we keep our basic information, where we invite our acquaintances. The people we really like, we invite to take off their coats and explore further. There's our library—that's where we keep our favorite ideas, beliefs, books, music, and movies. There's the garage, where we keep all the things we're working on, the projects we hope to send out into the world. There's our kitchen, where we keep all the things that feed our souls, like food and beauty and celebrations. There's the hall, where we keep the portraits of all the important people in our lives and the pictures of our favorite memories. There's the small room with the pretty view where we pray and read. There's the attic, where we put all the broken things in our lives, along with all the things we don't need anymore but hesitate to get rid of.

To really become friends with someone, we have to get past the front hall. But of course we cannot just storm around someone else's house investigating all the corners of their home; we must be invited into each room. I think a question is like knocking on the door. In the first weeks of grad school, all my classmates and I were making the same mistake: we were knocking on the front door, stepping in the front hall, taking a look around, and then leaving. We were asking questions that didn't open up the potential for further connection. By her simple question, my new friend showed interest in connecting. She knocked on the door of my library, and I invited her in, and a friendship was born.

This brings forward two principles we should consider.

First, we must make a habit of asking questions. This seems simple, but it is easily neglected. I have, from time to time, been shocked by conversations in which I was the only one who asked questions. I'm sure all of us have had those one-sided conversations where someone talks about herself, her opinions, and her day, with hardly a pause for a breath. Under the right circumstances, we all love to talk about ourselves, and it makes us feel closer to our conversation partner. That is important: talking about ourselves makes us feel closer to the person, but it doesn't necessarily make them feel closer to us. For both people to move towards closeness, there must be a sense of mutuality.

I once heard that a conversation ought to be like a tennis match: I serve the ball with a question, and you hit the ball back with a question for me. Think about questions like wandering through the other person's house. Perhaps you've taken a long time in the library, so why not knock on the door of the garage? If you are an internal processor and have a hard time coming up with questions on the spot, think ahead of time of some questions to ask. A good conversation is like an invigorating game, with each partner hitting back an interesting question. A conversation will get very boring if only one party always serves the ball.

So what do we do if someone never asks us a question? The first thing is that we mustn't attribute motives to their lack of questioning; the other person might be shy, insecure, or a narcissist! We cannot know, and it is not our business to judge. But I think that it is okay to acknowledge that not everyone will be our true, close friend, and if someone seems incapable of hitting the tennis ball back, she probably won't be. If, with a particular person, you find that your interactions consist solely of you asking all the questions, with her pouring out her heart while you are left feeling unknown, it's okay to not invest in that relationship. I have a five-question rule: I will ask five good questions, and then, if the other party does not respond, I quit. This isn't out of anger, just realism. I won't be able to have a friendship with someone who doesn't want to draw me out. If you find yourself in such a situation, bless the other person and be on your way, pursuing a friendship with more reciprocity.

This brings us to a second point: do not feel guilty for not investing in friendship with people who are drainers. You are not obligated to let anyone into the house of your heart. If someone never knocks, don't continue to pursue that person! If someone feels unsafe, pushy, or critical, you have every right to graciously back away from her. Now, this doesn't mean that you should throw out every relationship that is not beneficial or life-giving—certainly, being a follower of Jesus precludes this way of life. There are some relationships in which we will mostly be the givers; Jesus has modeled this for us, and we can do this with love and purpose. But when it comes to friendship, we should look for companions, kindred spirits who can give and take. This is not unloving; it is wise.

Compatibility: The Portrait of a Friend

So you have decided to be an initiator, to ask questions, and to pursue friends. But what sort of friend should you look for? What qualities should you seek? In his insightful book *The Four Loves*, C. S. Lewis sheds some light on the quest for friendship:

> The very condition of having Friends is that we should want something else besides Friends. Where the truthful answer to the question *Do you see the same truth?* would be "I see nothing and I don't care about the truth; I only want a Friend," no Friendship can arise—though Affection of course may. There would be nothing for the Friendship to be *about*; and Friendship must be about something, even if it were only an enthusiasm for dominoes or white mice. Those who have nothing can share nothing; those who are going nowhere can have no fellow-travellers.[2]

Lewis hits upon something very important here: good friendships are *about* something. And this is where they often differ from romantic relationships, which tend to focus more on the connection between two people (though they say that the greatest romances are sustained through friendship). From the beginning, my friendship with Elena has been about a dozen things other than just the two of us: at first it was about the common experience of college freshmen, it was about books and movies we loved, it was about the shared work of debate and classes and how we were going to manage toting all our groceries a mile back to our dorm room. Now our friendship centers on handling the new challenges of adulthood, reading and commenting on each other's writing, and sending each other recommendations for the best movies, shows, and books we've encountered recently (and videos of cute animals, if I'm honest).

Having common ground for what our friendships are about gives our relationships a center of gravity outside of ourselves. Friendships that revolve around filling all the emotional needs of one or both parties will buckle; friendships centered on something else, on the other hand, often fill emotional needs without becoming codependent. Commonalities are the suns around which we orbit in friendship; without them, there's no gravity to draw us together. But what sorts of things could or should our friendships revolve around?

My dear friend Abbie once said to me, "It takes a village to be a person." I think this is very good advice. We are complex people who need one another to draw us out in numerous areas of life. Rather than placing the expectations and needs of all areas of our lives on one friendship, we should take stock of the areas in which we are feeling lonely (heart? soul? mind?) and seek out friendships in those areas. We should take stock of ourselves and seek people who are compatible in heart, soul, mind, or strength.

So let's begin exploring various commonalities that can serve as suns for your friendships to orbit around.

I think of the heart as the world of our emotions, enjoyment, and story. Heart friends are those with whom there is a natural fondness, an ease, a delight. These are often the friends who check in on our emotional life, the things going on in our hearts—the friends who are attentive to the weather of our souls. What we share in these friendships is an appreciation and concern for the well-being of the other person. These relationships orbit around an interest in the journey of the person and their condition along the way.

I think of the soul as our values, beliefs, spirituality, and passions—the deeply rooted parts of us that make us who we are and shape our decisions and purpose in life. My soul friends are the ones with whom I can talk late into the night about my relationship with God, my hopes, and my doubts. These friends and I tend to think the same things are important, worth consideration, and worth discussion. They do not look askance at me when I talk freely about my prayer life, my convictions, and my sense of purpose and direction, because they're thinking about those things too.

Mind friends are the ones who share the things that occupy our thoughts and curiosities, the things we devote time to considering, researching, and keeping up with. My friend Jenna once told me, "Earnestly pursuing knowledge and truth will bond you with someone like nothing else." I think this is true; there is nothing like the pleasure of a rich, interesting, and easy conversation. Some of my favorite friendships began over a voracious appetite for intellectual and imaginative growth. This sort of friend is not just for the intellectual or academic; we all ought to cultivate a life of the mind, whatever that may look like for each person. We all ought to be interested in something, a master of some subject.

Strength friends are friends we make because of shared

activities. Doing things together—whether that's working, study-ing, playing, performing, or participating in charity events—gives us a shared experience to bond around. I've found that having an activity tends to take away the self-consciousness we some-times experience in relationships. As Lewis notes, an enthusiasm for dominoes can create a stronger bond than you'd expect. And the closer those activities get to who we are as people and what we are called to, the closer those friendships can become. My most meaningful friendships have begun around ministry (doing good for others), study (pursuing truth together), and work (accom-plishing meaningful goals together).

These categories are not comprehensive, but I hope they will provide some clarity about what we should look for in a friend-ship and perhaps what areas we may be lacking or feeling lonely in. I think that our best friendships ought to be a matrix of these categories, spilling over into one another. But I also have some deeply meaningful relationships that revolve around just one of these areas. Thinking in terms of these categories has helped me be realistic about the pressure I can tend to put on a friendship by wanting it to fill all the needs of my heart, soul, mind, and strength. It reminds me that no one but God is capable of filling all those needs in my life.

Commitment: Companions on the Road of Life

Now you have decided to date your friends. You've started to see yourself as an initiator, intentionally pursuing deep friend-ships. You've become practiced in the game of conversation and question-asking; you know how to politely knock on the door of someone's life. You are wisely and graciously guarded about who enters the house of your friendship. You've learned what to look for in a good friend and how to identify what sun your friendship orbits around. What's next? How do you move forward?

At this point in my friendship with Elena, what I find most precious is the years we have spent as companions in life. The spark of friendship, ignited at our mailbox meeting, has grown into a steady, reliable, warming fire. This connection came about because somewhere along the way we both realized we could count on each other. This boiled down to two keys that are essential when we think about dating our friends: rhythms of communion and covenantal commitment.

First, we had rhythms that ensured we'd see each other, connect, and catch up on all the important things in life on a regular basis. On a very basic level, having this designated time together bonded us simply because we developed a camera roll of memories, habits, and jokes together. But it also ensured that we could keep up on all the important things happening in each other's lives: the difficulties we were facing, the books we'd read, the jobs we were applying for, the things that made us laugh. As our lives have changed, this regular time has looked different. In college, no matter how busy we were, we went to the same grungy coffee shop every Friday to get a croissant and a latte and talk about our lives. Now we have regular Skype dates and are almost always planning the next time we'll see each other. We joke that "everything is a prelude" to our next reunion.

Second, somewhere along the way we decided we were each other's people. Whatever came, be it trial or triumph, we would be there to comfort or to celebrate. I think of this as something of a covenant. A covenant is a biblical idea, which involves binding yourself to someone through a commitment. Unlike a contract, you enter a covenant not out of self-interest or with the possibility of opting out when things are unpleasant but for the good of the other and as a commitment to stay together through thick and thin. I'm not going anywhere, and neither is Elena. There will be times when I need more than her or she needs more than me, or times when we're busy and can barely talk. But inevitably we return to that steadiness that comes from a committed friendship. As with a romantic relationship, a commitment to a friend takes years, trust, and a special bond. But what a comfort it is to know you have a friend you can lean on. There is nothing as sweet and good as a friendship that has withstood the years, a friend who has seen your eyes sparkle with both tears and excitement.

Elena is a treasure of a human being, and I am deeply thankful to have her friendship in my life. Our friendship has been a gift, but it has also been the fruit of intentionality on both our parts. As you pursue covenant friendship in your own life, I pray that you, too, might know the delight and satisfaction of a kindred spirit like Elena.

And come to think of it, I owe Elena a phone call.

CHAPTER 7

The Faithful Friend

*There is no possession more valuable
than a good and faithful friend.*

SOCRATES

SALLY ✺ God often delights His children with surprises
that remind us of His constant, generous love. Moses was tending
sheep when he saw the burning bush. The shepherds were in the
fields when a gathering of angels appeared in the night sky. The
Lord drew back the spiritual curtain, and Elisha saw Elijah swirl-
ing into heaven on a chariot of fire. An angel appeared to Mary
when she was probably doing something ordinary, such as washing
dishes or working in the garden.

The interesting similarity in each story is that each time God
appeared, people were not doing anything exceptional. He came
in ordinary moments, when those who were aware of Him were
in the midst of their daily rhythms.

In an exceedingly stress-filled season, the Lord pulled back the curtain for me, too, and let me glimpse the miracle He had been performing in my life over the years. It was one of those seasons during which I had felt alone and a little weary of work and travel. This was the fourth national hotel conference I was hosting in six weeks, in the midst of launching a book. I was wondering if my work was making a difference or not. That's when God flashed a series of memories through my mind, reminding me of His profound love and care through moments of ministry I had forgotten to notice.

When you glimpse such profound beauty, your soul is filled with deep awe and gratitude that you don't even know how to express. You can only bow in worship inside your heart, where no one else sees. Such was this span of a few short moments when God allowed me to see that years of heart and soul labor mattered. And while all of this was happening, no one in my audience even knew I was experiencing holy ground on the carpet of a hotel riser.

Every time I stand up to speak, adrenaline surges through my body, leaving me as jittery as a girl on her first date. Even after forty-two years of speaking at women's conferences and events, the surge of nerves has become a familiar experience to me.

Seeking to calm myself as I stood at the podium at our final Mom Heart conference for the year, I focused on the hundreds of women standing at round tables singing the words of a worship song with heartfelt passion. I could almost feel them breathing out the stress of the day and seeking to breathe in the calm the song promised. The feat of packing their bags, preparing food for their families, saying numerous good-byes to their children, and then flying or driving all the way to our hotel was what they all had in common. This would be a weekend of life-changing messages with kindred spirits all around and the promise of new friendships to be forged.

Thirty-five states and four foreign countries were represented at these tables, my assistant had informed me in a hushed voice. *Quite amazing*, I thought, *that women would come so far to gather with like-minded women.* A whisper-prayer to God to soothe my nerves and to give me the grace to see inside the hearts of these precious ones gave me something to focus on through the last two verses of the song before I began my talk.

Twenty-one years of Mom Heart conferences had taken me to this point. My husband, Clay, and I had dreamed up the vision for creating a conference where weary women, especially mamas, could get away for the weekend. There were to be messages of grace for these women who gave so much, inspiring talks to remind them of their strategic role in shaping a legacy of faith in their children. We longed for them to embrace the work of preparing their children to become adults who would carry the message of Christ to their generation. And I insisted on chocolate at each table. "We have to host them in hotels, so they can sleep on crisp, clean sheets and be in a professional environment. And we need to have a fun café where they can eat delectable food." Clay agreed!

Now, twenty-one years after we took a risk to rent our first hotel and ballroom, I was almost breathless to realize what God had accomplished through these amazing gatherings of friends. As I looked out over the crowd, I was suddenly aware of the gift these conferences had been to me.

Community with like-minded women is usually built slowly, one brick at a time, on a house that can eventually become a sanctuary to hold the love of kindred spirits and seasoned friendships. It grows slowly over years, creating a safe place where we can feel deeply, through those around us, the love, mercy, grace, and support of God. Such a community of affection and encouragement is worth the hard work of building over many seasons. And that is what God wanted to remind me of as I stood peering out in that moment.

It was then that God began to lift the curtain so I could see beyond surface-level recollections. First, I glanced to my side and saw my sweet friend Lynn. Appreciation and affection for her surged through me. Words of gratitude would never be enough to thank God for providing her on this journey. She had been with me every year for all twenty-one years of these conferences. She traveled with me, at her own expense, to the places I spoke. She was my helper in every way: carrying bags and hauling book boxes, shopping for medication and snacks when we had needs and wishes on the road, renting cars to drive me around, and in the early days, holding Joy as a baby while I spoke. Standing on her feet for hours at a time, behind book tables groaning with the weight of hundreds of recommended books, she patiently prayed with sweet women, told them about authors, and pointed out age-appropriate books for their children. I never asked her to do any of this, yet out of her own vision for our work, her personal faith and integrity, and out of loyal friendship to me, she gave tirelessly for more than two decades.

Lynn had been with me from the very first moment we gave words to the ideas shaping in the imagination of our hearts. We dreamed of building a ministry that would inspire parents to love and disciple their children. She was present at our first conference of just eleven people. This dear friend, now seventy years old, was standing with me in support as she had done for twenty-plus years. Other friends had come and gone as a result of different seasons of life, too many other commitments, and other reasons they needed to move on. But through all the years, Lynn had never left my side. Her commitment had cost her in time, work, sleepless nights, finances (to fly and to stay in hotels), and countless hours on the phone to encourage me. "Steadfast friend" is what I dubbed her in my mind as these thoughts flew through my head. She has stayed the course and kept the faith through all our years of building this ministry together. Everyone needs those steadfast friends who keep loving and giving because they have committed to do so, regardless of whether we deserve it or not. And maybe each of us needs to commit to being that kind of friend to others too.

Lynn and I first met at the playground in a park when our oldest children were seven and eight. These were the years in which I was becoming passionate and idealistic about the profound importance of motherhood. Messages seemed to flow into my heart every day when I had a quiet time and read my Bible.

Starting a moms' support group, I began to teach these principles of discipleship, and Lynn was always there, sitting in the back row listening intently and taking notes. *This is the way I want to teach and mentor my kids*, she thought in her heart. And from this small beginning, we became fast friends. I directed a musical in which her young son had the lead and my children had solos when they were eight, seven, and five, so the experiences we shared began to mount from the first year. The McDonald's playground was one of the places our children became friends while we chattered like magpies—about life, books, finances, messages, possibilities, travel, marriage, and heart issues.

We lived in the Nashville area at the same time for only a year and a half. My life would take me all over the United States, and her husband found a new job in North Carolina. Yet the fire had been lit in our hearts to be faithful friends through all our years. We challenged each other to start groups where we would faithfully teach messages to young women from the books I was writing. Eventually I grew my own family and simultaneously a ministry that encompassed twenty books (at this point), more than sixty national conferences for thousands of women, eleven years of blog posts, more than three million podcast downloads, and thousands of miles of travel—all because we wanted to serve Jesus by encouraging mothers. Together we believed that children are especially on the heart of Jesus, and we wanted to help mamas understand that.

As the melodic voices continued, I glanced around the room and realized that there were probably more than two hundred women in the room who had attended one of the small groups Lynn had taught over the years.

Then my mind flashed to literally hundreds of other faithful women. God painted a mental picture of what heaven will be like, when we will somehow see the beauty of lives poured out behind closed doors, while all along He saw every tiny and hidden gesture of faithfulness.

The meaningful friendships in my life show what can happen when lives are given and poured out for the benefit of another who needs love. And I believe God will use you in a similar way as you extend your love and time to others. Each woman who has befriended me over the course of almost thirty years of ministry came to me because of her integrity, her initiative to help, and her willingness to love others.

At first, there was Kathy, who was willing to dream with me and work hard to see our conferences become a reality. She and I would visit various hotels to try to figure out how to put the events together while making financial ends meet. Her children and mine served at registration tables and book tables and in countless other ways as we traveled across the United States together—nine of us in her Suburban. God also knew I would need practical help for all the details on the home front. He gave me the best next-door neighbor in the world, Shelley, who made us meals, traveled to all the conferences, entertained my kids, and stayed by my side through all the crazy years.

At each table were lovely floral decorations generously made and prepared by other faithful friends. They said it was a small way to give back after having their lives changed through one of our conferences, books, podcasts, or Bible studies.

Glancing beyond the crowds, in a screen across my mind, I traveled to numerous states—Colorado, Texas, California, North Carolina, Tennessee, Kentucky, Indiana, Oregon, and many others. I calculated that over the years, countless hundreds of women had exquisitely decorated tables and ballrooms. They had registered thousands with smiles and encouragement, often taking time to pray with those who were especially discouraged, carrying suitcases and diaper bags for women whose arms were full, holding their infants and toddlers.

And then there was my precious friend Lisa, back in Nashville, who for twenty-six years had continued the support group I had started where I had first met Lynn. She kept on year after year, teaching moms, organizing children, and watching generations of women come and go—a miracle of her own making. Then there was Marla, who had been serving for many years too.

My mind filled with deep gratitude as I reflected on my current "dream team," whose work reached far beyond me to remote places all over the world, through social media, podcasts, marketing, newsletters, and viral sharing. The influence of the ministry has grown because they work tirelessly to get the messages out, knowing I could never accomplish as an individual what our team has accomplished. Misty, Jennie, Gretchen, Kristen, Terri, Holly, Brandee, Ginger, Jacqui, Jessica, and my other amazing contributors have created the most beautiful and inspiring membership site. And amid their own hours of work, each took time to encourage me through my busy days. Deep friendship flows between us as we work together, though we live thousands of miles apart.

And how could I forget Sarah Mae, Angela, Kat, Ruth, Chrystal, and so many other bloggers and message makers who have partnered with me? So many faces marched through my thoughts.

Another memory flowed. My friend Beth had called me when she was a total stranger and said she wanted to start conferences in California. That small gesture of reaching out to me has borne many years of conferences attended by thousands of women in California. At the end of each conference, Beth hosted my family in her home for a Mexican fiesta she lovingly cooked. Then Sandra became a part of this gathering, and she brought floral arrangements, gathered my leaders in her home for appreciation luncheons and teas, and prayed for the attendees. She boldly shared her story to encourage the women and has continued a teaching ministry for years.

Jeanna joined us and said, "I will personally take responsibility for decorating all the tables at the Possibiliteas and making the room beautiful." My amazing Texas team followed suit, making everything more beautiful and hospitable. My leadership team in Colorado served tirelessly at conferences and in my home leadership intensives, where we fed up to fifty women for three days as they received training. They and their precious daughters cooked, cleaned, set tables, made floral arrangements, and washed dishes. I will never be able to repay them for their hard work. Shelley, Brandee, Stacy, Micala, Denise, and Margaret gave so much of themselves, as did those leaders who attended from all over the United States and beyond. How dear these women have become. And now there is Jacqui in England, Barb in Australia, and my sweet friends there. Until heaven, I will never be able to understand all the lives that intertwined because of the hearts of so many to reach out through this ministry we shared together. What a miracle it is to gather as women over common passions and messages.

There was also my launch team—"the best in the business," as several leaders in publishing have told me. For each book, my team crafted posters, shared on social media, gave gifts, and made generous use of their time to help spread the lifegiving messages. "How did you find such women?" many people have asked me.

This behind-the-scenes army of women used their creativity, energy, and words to inspire, encourage, and affirm women all over the world. The tapestry of thousands of women threading through the years created a masterpiece reflecting the beauty of committed friendships, the fullness of which will be revealed in eternity. I could never have imagined how reaching out and taking initiative would plant a harvest of deep relationships beyond my imagination.

As I travel this reminiscent journey, I am reminded of so many precious friends who have become gifts of love from the hands of God. I am sure to leave out some of my precious friends, because at sixty-five, I find that details are not my biggest strength. But you know who you are and how much I love and appreciate you for the ways you have loved me faithfully, comforted me in my discouragement, served tirelessly through the years, and kept the vision of helping encourage women through the messages we all hold dear. I will never forget your acts of love and the kindness you have shown in giving me your friendship.

This I know: there is a special kinship, an emotional and spiritual connection when people work together for a great cause. Soulish connections with so many women have enriched my heart and expanded the borders of my understanding in ways that have totally transformed my life.

Bonds of deep friendship are often forged when we join arms and move boldly to exercise our powerful influence. As I always say, women were made to civilize—and groups of women joining together as friends can move mountains.

And so, that day at the Mom Heart conference, when I began to speak, I was no longer thinking about my nerves or my inadequacy. Instead, my heart was filled to the brim with love to give back to all who filled the corridors of my memories.

Years ago, there's no way I could have guessed that these women who started out as strangers would become my closest of friends. And I never imagined I would have the privilege of sharing the thoughts, dreams, heartaches, and accomplishments of these precious women. We had bonded together around a common cause: helping women love, educate, cultivate faith, and pass on the message of Jesus to those in their lives. They were young and old, from every kind of background, with stories as varied as the places they had come from. What a privilege it was for me to become a part of the lives of so many vibrant, interesting women. In the context of coming together to encourage one another, we had joined hearts and histories.

In that moment, as I stood at the podium, love was invisibly pouring from my heart towards all these women, and I wished I could personally thank them for all they had given. None of this would have been possible if my sweet friends, like Lynn, had not joined arms with me to step out in faith to give themselves to building what is now an international movement. Over the past several decades, I have experienced the miracle of deep, soul-satisfying friendship that comes from people gathering around the same cause, the same higher purpose. My heart holds a deep well of treasures of love and memories because these women were willing to come together and to serve, shoulder to shoulder.

Serving and taking the risk to reach out are the foundation upon which these kinds of friendships are built. They are available to each of us.

The best and deepest friendships are formed through work accomplished together, serving others side by side. There is something special about sharing history, walking through life with one another, enduring the storms of life, and emerging as golden friends. This is how we build camaraderie—the deep friendship we all long for but so seldom find in this isolationist world. It requires commitment; formative relationships are created when we take the risk of meeting people who are at first strangers and then reach out to give love.

As the last verse of the last song pulsed to an end, I glanced over at my sweet friend Lynn, who was also singing. Now, I realized, my nerves were calmed. My heart was overflowing with deep gratitude for the steadfast friend she had been to me through so many years and through every type of situation: calamity, flourishing ministry, broken relationships, illnesses, separations, and new horizons where we started new ministries. She was my faithful friend. And we had both met hundreds of other women who had made all of this possible—friends who were willing to serve together and take the risk of always making moves of faith to ponder how we could reach more women and encourage them along their paths.

Somehow I had never consciously counted all these blessings that had passed through my life. Time had passed so swiftly through all the busy years. But at that particular moment, knowing the season of our Mom Heart conferences was coming to an end created an atmosphere of gratitude as I saw a small glimpse of what God had so faithfully provided.

This experience of walking through the years with so many kindred spirits was an unexpected gift, an experience of friendship I never could have planned or known how to create on my own. God granted me a gift that I think is waiting for women in every generation, every walk of life, when we invite, gather around heavenly purposes, and take the initiative to meet and serve together. It takes a willing heart and devoted commitment, but a life full of shared stories is just waiting to happen.

Shaping Communities of Friendships

Pondering the philosophy of ministry that Jesus lived out and taught is a worthy exercise. Because God desires relationship with us and created us for love, it is only a natural consequence that He planned to reach the world through groups of people who gathered around His own love and purposes to serve others and to find deep, satisfying community along this proven way. I think of the disciples—such a motley crew—living, serving, eating together—and how strong their bonds were because they were all willing to leave their fishing nets to follow Jesus.

Jesus walked the roads of His life as a commoner, a man who

had to eat and sleep, pay taxes, and work for His living. Rubbing shoulders with neighbors, family, and leaders in His community happened through daily life. And yet He gathered willing men and women around Him as those who would be His best friends—His closest companions who would eventually take His ministry and message to the whole world.

Jesus' first followers were people who longed for purpose beyond their mundane lives. "Come, follow me, and I will show you how to fish for people!" He told them (Matthew 4:19). Basically, His message to those in the small town where He lived was "Drop your nets and come with me to learn and serve." Something stirred in their hearts, and they responded. Their lives were forever changed by the decision to take a risk to follow this captivating rabbi.

Like me, they could not have known in those first days when they chose to be with Jesus and to invest their lives in His call just how much their borders would be expanded. At first, their interest was awakened to follow. Eventually, the call of Christ became profound, encompassing their whole lives as they became leaders in a worldwide movement. And yet it all started in such a small arena, close to home. And this became possible because they were willing to respond to Jesus' call to "follow me."

I love to imagine how deep and gratifying the friendships of Jesus' disciples became as they lived, moved, and learned from Him together. As they stood amid the thousands who came to hear Him, rocked in stormy seas on a small boat, and swallowed delectable fish freshly grilled over a beach fire, their shared experiences must have mounted up inside to create a treasure chest of memories. Surely they wrote letters, sought times to gather together, made room to share meals and memories the rest of their lives. This band of followers was bound together for life as a result of their common experiences. And so we see that deep friendship and community are the by-products of following Jesus' model of ministry.

One of the best ways to cultivate lifelong friends is by living, loving, and serving together. And what does this look like in day-to-day life? Here are three practical ways I've discovered to form friendships around ministry.

Take Action

Jesus left an admonition for all who follow Him to go into the world. The first step towards becoming connected to like-minded friends is to take action. We must go, join, attend, find a group that shares the same values or purposes that call to our own hearts.

Because each woman's personality and drive vary, different people might find like-minded fellowship in very different places—for example, you might experience connection by studying and reading books together, finding friends who care about education and starting a discussion group, hosting a Bible study in your home, or organizing a dinner group around subjects that engage minds and convictions. Or you might connect with others around shared experiences such as hosting international students, serving at homeless centers, leading a teen Bible discussion group, counseling at a crisis pregnancy center, hosting groups for encouraging moms, visiting the elderly, or building a ministry with women in prisons. There are endless ways to connect. But the first step is going—taking the initiative to join a group or to lead a group. Don't wait for someone else to reach out to you or ask you to join a group; be willing to take the first step.

Be Consistent in Loving Others

One of the most comprehensive verses in Scripture about friendship was given by Jesus as He instructed His disciples on the night of His crucifixion: "There is no greater love than to lay down one's life for one's friends" (John 15:13).

My life has required more work than probably anyone except my sweet children know. Speaking, standing in long lines to talk to women at the end of conferences, writing literally thousands of pages of encouragement through books and blogs, planning and recording podcasts—all of these grew out of a love for my Jesus and a passion to be a part of His Kingdom work.

Laying down our lives is not dependent on how someone responds to us or how well they serve us. Jesus said the greatest kind of love is to put aside our own needs so we can give, serve, and love. All of us are prone to pettiness, criticism, and having our feelings hurt—especially in women's groups, which include a variety of personalities and maturity levels.

Over the years of serving with women, I have learned that love covers a multitude of sins, that grace and forgiveness are the standards of Jesus' heart, that loyalty and steadfastness are choices we can each make, that all of us are flawed in our personalities and limited in our abilities, but that unconditional love gives us a bond that ties our hearts together.

I have found that there are so many others who are willing to work hard, lose sleep, and give generously as we work side by side. I love working with my friends who are as passionate as I am and even more adept at administration than I could ever be. And we have learned to love one another with all of our flaws and warts.

A Need for Balance and Rest

Jesus set an example for us by prioritizing rest and getting away. When He observed that His disciples were getting weary, He said to them, "Let's go off by ourselves to a quiet place and rest awhile." There were so many people around them that they didn't even have time to eat. Scripture says, "They left by boat for a quiet place, where they could be alone" (Mark 6:31-32).

A part of my growth from immaturity to maturity came from learning a balance between laying down my life to serve and setting appropriate boundaries. I began to notice when I was becoming impatient with others, resenting them because I had not learned to make those boundaries. In those moments, my friends told me, "I am not leaving you, Sally! I am here through your moods, rantings, apologies, and growth. You need to stop taking book contracts and speaking events. You need to get away. Let's plan a fun weekend together."

Having been subject to my own pity parties, I have had to realize that when I am weary and feel like the whole world needs me, I am likely to become critical of others. This sin habit is one I have learned to recognize in myself. I have learned that if I pay attention to my physical needs when I feel this way, I am able to become more loving again. A night of sleep, a week at home with few commitments, a happy movie, reading time, a warm bath, a massage, and time to be alone are some of the things that restore me. I also need time to refresh my soul by being with friends, enjoying and celebrating life together without even talking about ministry. I have learned to not take my varied emotions too seriously but to look inside and ask myself what is creating strife or dissatisfaction. When my friends have helped me pay attention to my own self, I have found I am better able to love and to return to the commitment to lean into patience and acceptance towards the very people I criticized.

As Jesus laid down His life, His rights, and His own needs for His friends, so we are called to do the same. This habit takes practice and self-patience and must be balanced with pulling away at times. This cycle of learning and grace comes with time and experience.

Learn to Bear with Others

Close friendships do not happen easily, and they don't necessarily happen naturally over time. There have been times in my life when I met someone who immediately became a best buddy. Yet usually friendship grows over time when planted in the soil of life, grown over seasons, and watered with love so it can flourish in the sunshine of life shared.

Many of my best friends became such because we have known each other for many years and invested in life together. A mature friend is someone who knows how to be a friend and how to be committed before the relationship has had time to grow.

When my children were very young, they would often fuss and say, "She was unfair. She took my toy!" or "He got the bigger piece!" or "She got the best toy!" (or any number of variations on this theme).

At times this childish fussing would drive me crazy. Yet I realized that I needed to help my children cultivate and practice mature love.

When they were especially prone to complaining against one another or felt they were martyrs while the other person was quite unjust, I decided to have them memorize some verses that have carried me through many relationships of my own. Though this is a long passage, I can now see the benefit of storing the words and meaning in all of our hearts, including my own, and key phrases from this passage are frequently on my children's lips. Whether you are cultivating relationships within your family or with your friends, it is a great guide to strong relationships.

Let love be without hypocrisy. Abhor what is evil; cling to what is good. Be devoted to one another in brotherly love; give preference to one another in honor; not lagging behind in diligence, fervent in spirit, serving the Lord; rejoicing in hope, persevering in tribulation, devoted to prayer, contributing to the needs of the saints, practicing hospitality.

Bless those who persecute you; bless and do not curse. Rejoice with those who rejoice, and weep with those who weep. Be of the same mind toward one another; do not be haughty in mind, but associate with the lowly. Do not be wise in your own estimation. Never pay back evil for evil to anyone. Respect what is right in the sight of all men. If possible, so far as it depends on you, be at peace with all men.

ROMANS 12:9-18, NASB

Reading this passage has always given me comfort, knowing that even the early Christians championing Christ needed to be reminded to be kind and humble, to not keep grudges, to reach out to people who were different from them. Even—and sometimes especially—in ministry, we are reminded of the humanness of people: we all get into arguments, we disagree, we get tired, we have different personalities. But somehow God uses us anyway.

Now, miracle of miracles, my children are each other's best friends. They get along (most of the time) and have a grand time together because for years their souls were shaped around the same values. They sipped the same favorite brand of tea every afternoon, and they shared the same music, authors, food, and chores! After building their friendship over many years, they are now able to fully appreciate each other's differences and personality quirks.

Of course, not every friendship has the bonus of being forged within the bonds of a family. But the same principles apply: we still choose to be devoted to our friends and to love them with brotherly love.

⌒⊙⌒

As I looked around me at the conference that day, I was deeply thankful for every woman I had enjoyed walking beside in ministry throughout the years, especially Lynn. Our hearts have grown close and our bond has grown strong because we have been tied together over the things that are most important to us. From sharing ideals about how we would raise and educate our children, to encouraging each other to walk with the Lord even through difficult seasons, to taking up our callings to mentor younger women, our friendship has been about something bigger than us, so it lasted.

Just like in the parable that admonishes us to build our lives on a rock, on a foundation of things that won't wash away with time (Matthew 7:24-27), this friendship is built on a rock because what it is centered on will not wash away with the sands of time.

If you have a faithful friend like Lynn in your life, thank God for this rare gift, and recommit to making that friendship a priority, whether that means writing a letter of appreciation to that person or scheduling a visit or a phone chat. If you are longing for such a faithful friend, ask God to show you how to *be* a faithful friend—how to take the first step and then to show consistent love and bear with your friend, whatever may come.

Maybe God has called you to be a Lynn—one who is committed to holding up the arms of another whose arena is too big for one alone to bear. No matter what your personality or your calling, consider whether God is nudging your heart to become a faithful servant in reaching out to others or serving with others in a group that God has especially put on your heart. It is my hope that you, too, will find the surprise of deep friendship forged in committing to a purpose bigger than yourself and that in doing so, you, too, will find heart satisfaction.

CHAPTER 8

Looking for Avonlea

Everything that's worth having is some trouble.

L. M. MONTGOMERY

SARAH When I was a child, I wanted to live in Avonlea.

Avonlea is the tiny village in Prince Edward Island where the characters of my favorite books (the Anne series by L. M. Montgomery) and my family's favorite show (*Road to Avonlea*, Kevin Sullivan's production based on Montgomery's books) lived in delightful, funny, endearing community. To me, Avonlea meant the fellowship of the King family, an opinionated and fiercely loyal bunch of siblings and cousins who fought and celebrated and learned and grew together. There were the King cousins—Felix, the entrepreneurial middle boy; Felicity, the bossy and brilliant older sister; Sara, the "story girl" of vivid imagination; and gentle-hearted Cecily. And there was the circle of wise adults who surrounded them—the stringent and idealistic Aunt Hetty, the wise and kindly Uncle Alec, the feisty and compassionate Aunt Janet, and the dreamer Aunt Olivia. Avonlea meant a community woven of loyal, difficult, delightful people who stuck together through the years of farming or teaching, writing or dreaming, their lives and work rooted in the soil of their place on earth. Avonlea meant the joy of watching the seasons change, of children growing, of houses settling into the earth a little more deeply each winter, of the apple trees planted at each child's birth finally bearing fruit.

We Clarksons loved the tales of Avonlea. We savored them together, those short episodes with their images of ordinary drama: Christmas feasts and sibling squabbles, petty fights and forgiveness, gardens planted and homes built. The word *Avonlea* became our shorthand for community, for that sense of rooted belonging that grows over the years between people who love each other and their place with a long, creative love. As a child, I saw Avonlea as something to simply be celebrated, a story that reflected my own deep joy in my family and the world. We Clarksons were like the Kings; we ate and feasted and grew and fought. We loved each other fiercely and had our own set of high ideals and strong personalities, and our home (wherever it currently was) felt like its own small town because we all belonged. We were, all told, a merry little fellowship of our own.

But sometime in my early teens, after another move to a new state, the word *Avonlea* began to have a wistful sound to it; I began to recognize the hunger at the heart of our family's love of Avonlea as we started over in a new place and strove to create friendships and community, to find a church one more time. I looked at our own family traditions and began to realize that my mom watched *Avonlea* with a deep sense of yearning as she strove to create Avonlea in our home but had little help or companionship herself.

In my late teens, as the larger world drew me towards its sphere and I yearned for independence and like-minded companions, Avonlea began to be tinged with an almost painful hunger. I looked at the world I was entering, in its cool, contemporary bustle that seemed to draw me away from community, not into it, and wondered where in the world a life like the one in Avonlea could be found.

In my twenties, mired in the work and wrestle of trying to establish myself as an adult, of seeking a place to belong, to be known, to grow for many years to come, Avonlea became an ideal, something I knew was beyond my reach. I realized that in my moving from this church to that or this job with a student group to that one with a ministry, from a small American town to a big European city, I was searching for my own Avonlea.

But I wasn't at all sure if I would ever find it.

To be perfectly honest, I am still somewhat stymied about what it means to build and keep community. After almost five years in Oxford, I know this city so well, and yet I wonder if I am known in return. Do I deeply know the other souls who dwell here? Have I "arrived," in any real sense of relationship? These are my ongoing questions in this swift city, this swift world, my own busy life, and to my chagrin, I have to answer no in many ways. Community is still both my yearning and my hopeful work.

I spend my days as a young married woman, a new mother, living overseas and navigating a foreign culture in some of the most transitional moments of my life. I'm American, my husband is Dutch, and we live in England, both away from our beloved families and home cultures. Oxford, however much we love it, is one of the most transient places I have ever experienced; friendships are swift and often deep, lasting intensely for a year, and then . . . gone. But our life here might just be preparation for the decades to come. Thomas's vocation as an Anglican pastor/priest means it is unlikely we will stay anywhere for more than three or four years in the near future. And the membership of the Girls' Club is scattered all over the world. We girls couldn't even choose to move closer to each other if we wanted to, because none of us really knows where we'll be in another year, or even six months.

I know all of this, and yet community is one of my most deeply held, tenaciously sought ideals. I believe that human beings were made for profound connection. What do I mean by community? I mean the peace that comes from belonging—to a place, a people, a fellowship of believers and neighbors. I mean the joy of sharing your story with others who will be faithful to you as you are to them; of lives woven together over the years of work and grief and celebration. I mean friends with whom you can form and live a commonly held foundation of faith and moral action. By community I mean faithfulness, the knowledge that you are held in a love larger than your own and live in its daily companionship.

We glimpse this in the origin story of the world: look back to Eden, when the world was perfect and our hearts still whole, and what do you find? A home and a family. A garden carefully crafted by God Himself as the space of ultimate rest and flourishing. A man and a woman made to create an ever-expanding fellowship between themselves while keeping in perfect communion with their Creator. In Eden, we belonged. We were rooted in a place, known deeply by those around us and by God Himself, given purpose and work, and I believe that original identity is deeply etched into the human heart. We cannot escape it, for though the Fall exiled us, literally, from our original home and broke the trust and love that made the first community so joyous, we are haunted by a desire for that original home and first fellowship.

It's a yearning that is magnified in a global, technological world in which we no longer have a reason to stay in a single place long term, to know our neighbors or root in one corner of the earth. As a young adult, I have often felt that we live in a world that makes strangers of us all. Wendell Berry once called airports the "Gate of Universal Suspicion,"[1] because in them we are disconnected from anything that makes us known, that roots us to a particular place or people. There is no longer a common consensus about what is good or virtuous, and we struggle to find people to share our convictions, our beliefs, our faith. We live in a world of broken families and scattered communities, of children who don't know where home is and adults who carry the confusion and desire to belong into every decision we make. I think you can hear that sorrow pulsating throughout the modern world, in the yearning of breakup songs, in novels about the search for a home that can't be found, even in the cynicism and disillusionment so famously part of the millennial generation's outlook, a view I know too well sometimes myself.

How do we ever hope for connection in such a hopeless state of affairs?

The answer to that question is one I have been studying since my little-girl love for Avonlea, but especially in the past years as I have begun my roles as a wife and a mother. My current season of life has been marked by my need to come to terms with the fact that community for my family won't look like I imagined it always would. Last summer I found myself profoundly discouraged by the isolation of our Oxford lives. I had a miniature breakdown of pregnancy hormone–induced sobbing with my husband. At one year married, with a baby on the way, our future entirely uncertain, and our families far away, I felt I simply could not muster the energy or belief I needed to keep seeking connection; to continue opening our little home to another group of strangers; to seek, one more time, to create a real network of girlfriends when my own Girls' Club was so far away.

Thomas and a dear local mentor both challenged me to be honest in prayer about my struggle. They urged me not to deny or suppress it but to make it a conversation with the Holy Spirit. So I opened my heart and hands in a plea for the Almighty to get me back on my feet, to show me the way forward, to give me hope. Slowly, I found my courage afresh. I read Psalm 37, with its calm directive to "trust in the LORD and do good; dwell in the land and cultivate faithfulness" (verse 3, NASB). This psalm has shaped and convicted me throughout my adulthood with its challenge to create life in difficult places.

I read books about the way small, hidden lives of faithfulness and affection directly influence the ongoing goodness of the world. A friend visited me, bringing cinnamon rolls and tea, and the grace of that tiny act startled me with the sense of blessing it brought.

Moment by tiny moment, I heard the Aslan-whisper of "Courage, dear heart," and I came to a new grip on what it means not to wait for Avonlea but to create it in my own sphere of life. I began to understand what it might look like for me to turn my loneliness into faithfulness, to make my corner of existence an outpost of the Kingdom of Heaven.

What I finally grasped at the end of that summer is that the creation of community is an act of redemptive, holy defiance, one that is a lifelong work of artistry and love, one that costs everything we have to give.

I never expected friendship and fellowship to be so difficult to find; who does? But how can it be anything else? We live in this broken place, where sin and Satan wage war with God, and the battleground is our hearts, our loves, our fellowship with each other. Relationship, connection, communion—these are what Christ came to restore, and our work as His followers is to defy the disconnection and isolation of the world by being creators, by calling friendship and fellowship out of the lonely void, just as God spoke light into the darkness at the beginning of time.

I had been searching for community, but all along that was something I was actually called to create.

What does community look like, and how do we learn to create it? I've been learning that community can be boiled down to three powerful words, the same ones Paul chose to end his famous description of enacted love in 1 Corinthians 13: faith, hope, and love.

We must rekindle our vision for community by the sight that comes with faith.

We must live by hope and act in its creative energy.

We must endure in love and commit to staying in relationships for the long term.

Faith: Rekindled Vision

The first step to creating community is simply to believe that it is possible.

Sometimes this can feel almost impossible to do. The disconnection we have known often steals our vision for community, our will to imagine that we can love and be loved in faithful, long-term fellowship. But we cannot create what we cannot imagine. When I came to my place of discouragement last summer, I realized that I needed something to help me restore my faith, even my inner image, of what community could be. Bookish girl that I am, it's no surprise that my faith was restored by stories—two novels, to be specific: Wendell Berry's *Remembering* and Elizabeth Goudge's *Pilgrim's Inn* both gripped me by the hand and set me on my feet with a fresh faith in the possibility of community.

Wendell Berry's story describes a middle-aged farmer named Andy who comes to a crisis in a San Francisco hotel room, far from his Kentucky home. Isolated, estranged from his family by his anger and despair over an injury that changed his life, he finds himself struggling to believe that meaningful work and love are possible. What stops him in his path of self-destruction is simply a memory. As he stands on the Pacific coast, watching the sun rise, he remembers the vivid, dramatic stories he heard as a child recounting the lives and work, the hope and faith of his ancestors, the people who built the house and farm and town that are central to his identity, the people in whose faithful lives his own existence became possible. In remembering how they invested to create the community of which he is a part, he is "held though he does not hold."[2] His vision is restored. And from that moment he begins the journey home, back to the life of connection and love he will continue by returning to his wife and children.

Stories like this restore our vision. We remember right along with Andy that community is real and possible, even when we have been isolated and alone. That kind of narrative helps us to imagine what affection and laughter, good meals and traditions look like.

That's what the second book, *Pilgrim's Inn*, did for me too. I read it every year in the autumn because it is a rich and poignant tale of home. It's the story of how one English family, battered and broken by the loss and grief of World War II, find refuge in an old country home. They come, slowly, to a fellowship with one another as the old house draws them together. They work and relate, they fight and learn, they come to remember that, in Goudge's lustrous words, "Every home was a brick in the great wall of decent living that men erected over and over again as a bulwark against the perpetual flooding in of evil."[3]

In reading that line, I understood afresh that to create community is to fight the good fight of love as it invades the world in the coming of Christ. That story, with its account of the cooking and cleaning, the petty squabbles and peaceful moments, the evening feasts and fireside talks that constitute the good work of hospitality, enabled me to imagine what love in action might look like in my own life.

When Paul prays urgently for those to whom he writes that "Christ will make his home in your hearts as you trust in him" (Ephesians 3:17) so that they will be empowered "with inner strength through his Spirit" (verse 16), I think he is praying for restored imagination. He yearns for them to comprehend "how wide, how long, how high, and how deep his love is" (verse 18) because that vision is what will enable them to live "a life worthy of [their] calling" (Ephesians 4:1). This is why we are urged throughout Scripture to root ourselves in God's Word—because the fallen world continuously steals and deadens our vision, drains our hope, and dims our faith.

Remember the stories and reclaim the vision; this is the first work of a woman who wants to create community. We must so enrich the soil of our own souls and hearts that they become the place where the seeds of fellowship will grow. When I think of the women whose lives and homes are centers of community, where people are drawn out of loneliness and into friendship, I am struck by the fact that each of these women is nourished deeply by story and Scripture. Each feeds herself by continually rekindling her vision, her capacity to imagine love and picture how she will embody it in her own life. It's a simple step, but I have come to realize that it's crucial. To renew our minds, as described in Romans 12:2, is vital to the creation of community, because fellowship is one of the gifts a fallen world teaches us to despair of ever finding. We cannot create what we cannot imagine.

Hope: Creativity Renewed

The second step to becoming a creator of community is to live by the energy that comes from hope. Faith restores vision, and stories teach us what to imagine, but hope drives us to creativity, to actually craft the beauty we have seen. Hope is the power by which we make our visions real, enfleshing God's goodness right in the midst of a lonely, fallen world. I love Elizabeth Goudge for her plucky opinion that women are the ones with the power to "[make] the bricks"[4] of home and community, and I have seen this played out firsthand as I have watched my own friends and mentors create life in such a way that connection is made possible by hospitality, laughter, good traditions, and great feasts.

There are few things more beautiful to me than witnessing the small worlds of beauty and community that women make when they work in the power of hope, creating astonishing connections in their own small spheres. Last year, right about the time of my crisis, I visited Joy in her little gem of a room up in St. Andrews, where she was finishing up her master's degree. I stumbled off the train, bleary eyed and exhausted from pregnancy and weeks of study, and was instantly swept up in Joy's lively care. She had only a tiny student room with a bed, a desk, and a battered old pink chair, but the walls were dotted with prints and photos, and the window was framed in a line of fairy lights. She sat me down in that chair as if I were a visiting princess. She opened the windows to the ocean breeze, set her matchless indie music playlists to trilling, brewed me a cup of tea, and put a dark-chocolate digestive (a cookie, in American terms) in my hands. That room was tiny, but it was her small realm, and in it she was queen.

Joy opened her tiny space to all her friends in such a way that it was a center for hospitality (and a known outpost of good tea and biscuits). Movie nights and tête-à-têtes, deep discussions and study sessions, moments of prayer and hours of laughter—all this Joy brought into being by crafting her space and enacting love. What made her hospitality more poignant was the fact that I knew she was tired. She had been working nonstop on essays and deadlines, and there were times that she reached out when she was exhausted herself. But what I saw in Joy was the radiant life that comes from a heart filled with hope, with belief in the possibility of friendship, beauty, and connection. Because of that hope and what it drove her to create, Joy's initiative became the place where community began.

When we act in hope, when our lives enflesh our belief, we make the love of God and the coming of His Kingdom touchable, tasteable realities. Joy and countless other great women I have known see themselves as partners with the Holy Spirit. They nourish their hearts by Scripture, they enrich their souls by story, and they ask the Holy Spirit to quicken their minds with His own imagination. Their homes or dorm rooms, wherever they might be, become outposts of His Kingdom as they act in the power of His love.

Community isn't something that just happens. It has to be planned and crafted, worked at and scheduled. Community begins with a person who is willing to prepare the meal, invite the crowd, clean the house, put on the music, and light the candles. Community is not abstract; it happens in the here and now of the people around us (however imperfect) sharing the stuff of the ordinary and celebrating, suffering, and growing together.

More important, though, it begins with the stuff right at our fingertips. Community isn't about an ideal group of like-minded people we will meet someday or the home that will finally have enough space for a real party. It isn't about perfect people or ideal circumstances. It's about love taking the stuff of the ordinary and turning it into fellowship.

When I began to embrace this vision for community for myself, my husband and I sat down to think about how we could create community right in the midst of our own slightly hectic lives, in our little house (we can fit seven—count 'em now, seven—in our living room on a good night) with the highly diverse and quirky (we use this word to describe ourselves) people we know. We thought about the other people in our vicinity who, like us, might be yearning for connection while mired in busyness and without any real chance to be known. We made a list, planned a meal, and held the inaugural meeting for what we called STS—Surprise

Theological Society. Each week one member of our group would make a meal and another would bring copies of some piece of reading—theology, literature, poetry, philosophy—to read aloud for the whole group to then discuss. We prayed and we planned, and since STS began, it has grown into an unexpected fellowship of highly disparate souls who come together to share ideas and dinners.

Community requires that we ask ourselves the questions that become the building blocks of holy creativity:

- Who are the people God has given me to love?
- What do I have to offer?
- How will I make my own home a place of beauty and welcome?
- Whom will I invite?
- How will I help us to connect?

Questions like these are driven by the energy of hope as it works to enflesh love.

Love: The Long, Faithful Gift

Paul said it best: the greatest of these words is love. We can have vision, we can have hope, but love is the blood pulsing through the veins of our good plans. What do I mean by love? Love is the giving of ourselves, the gift of our capacity and time, our patience and our goodwill. Community requires that someone lay down her life. True community, the kind that lasts, requires someone to be the giver, to be the one who pours out the generous love that brings people and places to life and connection.

When I sat down to figure out how I, as a wife and mother, living apart from family, uncertain of the future, could learn to be a giver, one person came to my mind. Love, I realized, became real to me in my mom.

The thing is, I really did grow up in Avonlea. The only way I could have known to love that imagined, idealized vision of home and family, that image of community, was because I touched and tasted a bit of real fellowship every day in my own life. My mom made this possible through what I now recognize was the daily, faithful, generous pattern of action by which she poured herself out to create the community in our home and family that she so hoped to find for herself. She is an image to me of love and the long-term fellowship it creates.

She never had it easy; we moved every few years when I was growing up and lived far from family. She had little help, a lot of work, and only the rare bit of encouragement. But love, for my mom, meant that she didn't despise the tiny community of our family. She saw us kids and my dad as worthy of the gift of her whole self, and she gave generously, creating a sense of Avonlea-type belonging that profoundly shaped each of us.

My mom's love meant that each house we lived in became a place of beauty and rest. That didn't mean perfect upholstery and spotless rooms; love enfleshed meant bright pictures on the walls and music playing, candles lit in the evenings and cozy corners prepared for squirming little bodies who made messes in every room they touched. Love meant that the hours we spent together were formed by her attention to the traditions and rhythms that would help us to know we belonged, that we were known and at home. Love also entailed reading times that gave us a shared story, family dinners that knit our days together and helped us to know each other well, traditions that wove us into a story of faith and family, and prayer times that showed us what it meant to have fellowship with God.

Because of my mom's willingness to pour herself out in love, my family became the first community I knew, a gift that shapes the way I see the whole world. What's remarkable is that my mom didn't consider her children unworthy of her effort. Her love created the family fellowship that lasts now into our adulthood in friendship and shared convictions, in a sense of belonging undimmed by the many miles that separate us. Her love became the soil of the Girls' Club, and that love continues in the way Joy and I both strive to create community in our own lives, continuing my mom's faithful choice to give herself in creativity and love.

Love also meant that we saw our home as a place where other people were welcome. I complained as a teenager that we were always the ones who started groups and invited people to dinner (I resented this mostly because of the dishes it required me to wash), but as an adult I am grateful for the heritage I learned as my mom taught me to be a giver. In every city we lived in, we kept our tradition of a mother/daughter Christmas tea. We started a new book group. We had a Christmas open house and an autumn harvest festival. I thought it was all an immense amount of trouble at the time, but I now see that all the giving was making lifelong connections.

My mom's poured-out love continues in all of us as we love others and create community in our different corners of the world. Joy in Scotland, hanging fairy lights and brewing tea; Mom in Colorado or Oxford, playing her beautiful old music and writing away, her phone constantly ringing as each of us kids calls home in a ceaseless circle of conversation; me in Oxford with my Lilian, reading aloud and making our old family-favorite meals—we are a community. We do not have the grace, right now, of living near each other, and it's something we pray may happen someday. But spurred on by the belonging we have in each other even from afar, through texts and phone calls, letters and visits, we can reach out from these roots and create community in our own spheres. The invisible connection between us is expressed in the Tuesday group dinners that Joy joins and hosts for the women in her small town, in the teatimes my mom organizes for old friends and young women in need of mentoring, in the big discussions of faith and art that Thomas and I host in our home. We are always seeking to enlarge the circle of love that we first learned at home.

Rowan Williams, in his writing about the grace to be found in the novels of Dostoevsky, describes the presence of incarnational figures in certain stories. Those are the people who seem to make life possible in a different way. When they are present in their generosity and joy, their love and courage, the horizon shifts and forgiveness or beauty or joy becomes possible. When these people are present, as Christ was, a new story begins.

My mom was an incarnational figure, and I hope that I can be too, because I want my life to be the ground in which the stories of others begin afresh. I want my home and my days to be the space in which the story of a new community begins. But that can only happen if I learn to pour out my heart and effort, my life and joy in acts of love.

A huge shift of identity transpires when we begin to see ourselves not as waifs and outcasts *looking* for community but as agents ready to bring it to the lonely spaces we encounter. It has taken me most of my life to begin to understand what it means to live in love, to create community instead of demand it. But I'm getting there.

You see, I'm no longer looking for Avonlea.

I'm making it instead.

CHAPTER 9

The Tribe

In a perfect Friendship this Appreciative love is,
I think, often so great and so firmly based that each
member of the circle feels, in his secret heart, humbled
before all the rest. Sometimes he wonders what he
is doing there among his betters. He is lucky beyond
desert to be in such company.

C. S. LEWIS

JOY 🙾 Middle school girls have a surprisingly sophisticated caste system for popularity. During my middle school years, there were two girls in whose hands the scepter of social approval lay. Let us call them the Queens. At regular intervals, the Queens would adopt a girl. From one weekend to the next, she dressed, spoke, and ate like them. The turnover rate for "the girl" was high; she rarely became a permanent fixture. To my thirteen-year-old mind, it all seemed rather marvelous.

I was the girl for a week once. I knew because I was invited to a sleepover where I ate too much sugar, watched a stupid movie, and most certainly did not sleep. I was cajoled into saying which boys I thought were cute and which people I thought were annoying. I immediately felt a mixture of guilt (for criticizing people), fear (that they might tell the boys my opinions of them), and annoyance (I do not like being made to do things I wish not to). I felt like a spy, enduring a sugar-fueled sleep-deprivation exercise intended to extract gossip from me. If only my captors had known that when it came to gossip, I was a remarkably oblivious source.

It came as something of a relief when abruptly, and without explanation, I was no longer invited to the hallowed sleepovers. I went back to my best friend, who also wasn't in on their antics, and my bookish boys, and was a little lonely but mostly content.

Perhaps this snapshot of middle school existence reveals more about me than the social dynamics of women: mainly that I am a private person, I hate Skittles, and I truly hate pulling all-nighters. But it was more than that. What truly put me off was a foggy sense of danger and a fear of misstepping or misspeaking. Friendship with the Queens lacked depth, delight, and the pleasure of camaraderie, but it also felt dangerous. I felt like I ought to ask for a nondisclosure contract before I went home.

For much of my life, this is how I have experienced groups of women. With the exception of my own family and the excellent company of women my mother did ministry with, my experiences with groups of women were thoroughly underwhelming or off-putting. Again and again I found myself with that same sticky, unsafe feeling, being drawn into things that didn't feel like me, being bored. It seemed to me that, in an attempt to foster cohesion, groups often appealed to the lowest common denominator of similarity among everyone, which rarely amounted to much more than a sappy vacuity. And when groups of women didn't make me feel disenchanted, I felt wary. There is a cruelty that groups of women are capable of. Almost every woman I know has been burned by the fire of gossip. I was thoroughly pro female friends but thoroughly ambivalent towards groups of females.

That is, until I encountered the Tribe.

September 3, 2016, found Rebecca Moon (my oldest friend) and me standing guard over a small mountain of suitcases in a tiny Scottish bus station. Rebecca—a saint and a doll—met me in London to take the trek to Scotland and help me move into St. Andrews, where I was starting my master's program. After two days of helping me heft my bulging luggage on and off trains in the split second before the train left us or our belongings behind, Rebecca seemed to take on truly magical qualities in my mind.

Thank You, God, for Rebecca Moon, I thought as she deftly hailed a cab from the queue.

I had never stepped foot in Scotland before I moved to St. Andrews. I had never met any of the professors. Everything was new and unfamiliar. Rebecca was a lifeline as I was neck deep in unfamiliar, if not unfriendly, Scotland. She moved me in and then out of my first asthma-inducing apartment, hunted with me for a new one, moved me in again, and explored St. Andrews with me, all while I didn't even have a bed to offer her. As I said, a saint.

But Rebecca had to go home.

I remember sitting alone in my room, which was sparsely decorated with the few things I'd brought with me and still smelled strongly of new paint. A cocktail of trepidation, excitement, and anxiety bubbled in my stomach. What was I to make of this new life? And who was I to make it with?

Oddly, none of us remember exactly how we came together as a crew. We met through the divinity school, sticking out as a subset of two minorities: women and Americans. My room was the most central in town, so somehow we fell into the habit of congregating on my floor (I only had one chair) with a bar of chocolate and mugs full of something warm. We would laugh, lament, and dissect our days. We fell in with each other and never fell out. We happened upon our name when one of my Scottish friends asked whether I had plans for the upcoming holiday.

"You're probably doing something with that tribe of women you hang out with," he said.

"Why, yes. Yes, I am."

We needed each other. We'd all stumbled into this remote fishing village in Scotland and found ourselves fumbling our way around the British academic system and our burgeoning adulthood. Everything—and I mean everything!—was unfamiliar. From the way we cited our papers to washing our hands with scorching hot or icy cold faucets to buying groceries and going to the doctor, everything seemed difficult. And as we mastered looking the right way to cross the street, we were also lurching into academia, trying and sometimes succeeding to live into our new identities as grad students with something worth saying to the world. We needed each other to laugh with over the impracticality of tiny British washing machines, to puzzle over syllabi, and to buy a cake on one another's birthdays. We banded together out of necessity, but somewhere along the way, these people became the ones I wanted to call when something exciting, upsetting, or hilarious happened.

Those early months blend together in an impression of emotion: a growing sense of belonging. There's one early moment we all remember. One afternoon Rebecca, Jenna, and I encountered a beleaguered and visibly upset Macie. After some probing, she recounted the source of her unhappiness. While walking home after classes, she'd been poorly treated and bullied by a number of her male classmates. At once, the three of us became mother bears, responding with appropriate ire, sympathetic anger, and bracing hugs. We then puttered back to my house with the best medicine we could think of: fish and chips.

The Tribe to the rescue!

We began to count on each other. When one of us had the flu, the others brought medicine, food, and flowers. When a holiday or a birthday rolled round, one of us—usually Jenna—organized the celebration, assigning dishes and drinks to bring and coordinating schedules. When paper deadlines hovered over our heads, we checked in with each other. Has Joy eaten? When was the last time Jenna left her apartment? Has Macie slept? Has anyone heard from Rebecca? When someone had good news or got a good grade or received a scholarship, we went out, wearing heels and lipstick, and celebrated. When sorrow struck, we took turns visiting, cleaning, bringing food. And when we needed a study break, Jenna would walk by my open window and shout, "Joy!" beckoning me for a quick walk and chat. We were on call for companionship.

Now do not be mistaken. Our personalities do not fit together like puzzle pieces, nor do our stories. And with four strong personalities, there have been moments of tension (though in my memory, they mostly derived from my low blood sugar—sorry!). But the strength in all of us that can occasionally cause friction is also the strength that makes our bonds so strong and that makes me want to be a better person. The nourishment of my friends' company isn't just in belonging to a group but in the privilege of each woman's individual presence.

Let me tell you about them.

There is Jenna. Jenna is tall, lean, and upright. She has short dark hair, and according to the style of her native West Coast, she is always overdressed and understated. She walks quickly, like she has a destination, because she always does. When she stops to gaze at something, she leans neatly back on one well-placed foot in fourth position and assumes the attitude of the art curator coming to a well-informed decision about a painting. Behind her heavily lashed dark eyes roam many thoughts that are not expressed. Every motion of her body is on purpose, because everything Jenna does is on purpose. She cannot be compelled to do something she doesn't mean to do. But when she does choose to do something, she does it with extravagant excellence. Whether it's a masterful academic presentation or a Thanksgiving turkey or a painting of the St. Andrews skyline, there is an unmistakable deftness and beauty in every work to which Jenna applies her skill. What is given to Jenna is safe: keys, secrets, and sorrows. The most extravagant gifts of all are her gentleness and vulnerability, which are not won but granted. Jenna is true and good, always knows how to fix things, and always has a snack.

There is Rebecca. Rebecca is also tall. Rebecca has a profligacy of hair that sometimes appears red and sometimes blonde but always tumbles in untidy, glorious waves down her shoulders. She dresses beautifully and carelessly, a reflection of her sophisticated upbringing, her time working in retail, and her general desire to be at home reading a book. Though she is easygoing and unlikely to impose her will on a group, there is a blessed decisiveness in Rebecca; she is the best person to take shopping. She grew up in the Deep South and in Oregon wine country. Containing, as she does, so many diverse and sometimes opposing histories, there is space in Rebecca's world for all sorts, and she never seems surprised by anyone. She is quietly insightful and self-effacingly frank. I don't think that Rebecca sleeps, a fact that has probably enabled one of her other virtues: she has read more than almost anyone I know, and in this world of academia, I'm around a lot of readers. She is a daydreamer and an overthinker, but she is tied to the earth by her fearsome loyalty to friends and family, about whom she can spin warm and affectionate stories.

There is Macie. Macie was frequently mistaken for a European during her time in Scotland. She sports a French bob, the hue of which changes depending on the month. Macie's head is often tilted to the side, as though she's adjudicating a philosophical proposal or an emotional conundrum (and she often is—sometimes at the same time!). The movements of her gait are too dignified to be called wiggling but too fluid to be called striding; she has a whimsical elegance reminiscent of a cat. But do not be deceived: beneath her European charm is a piercing and agile wit and a probing, archival mind. During the summer when we wrote our dissertations, Macie read *War and Peace* "for fun." But do not be deceived, either, by the mind that is Macie, for she is also deep and tender. Macie is overwhelmed at times by the beauty and tenderness of the world, but she would not ask for less. She loves nothing better than to lie in the grass of a hidden garden, gazing at all the green and blue and loveliness and soaking in the rays of sun that will soon metabolize into the scattered freckles on her nose and her own palpable delight.

In each of these friends, I encounter a distinct world with a landscape all its own. Together we are a continent with friendly borders. They make me want to be more excellent, more careful, more tenderhearted. They make me want to read more, pray more, cook more, laugh more, take more walks, and love more. Each one of them is a large soul, a woman of great capacity. But there is space for us all—to be accepted, challenged, and celebrated. I am safe in these friendships, and called to goodness.

In the past I had known the uplifting amicability of one friend at a time, but never this glut of delight and edification. Where had such women been all my life?

The things with the greatest power for destruction have an equal capacity for good. Through my treasured friendship with the Tribe, I realized that many of the things that made my group friendships with women so trying and sometimes damaging were the very potentialities that can make societies of sisters so powerful.

In my experience, there are three main roadblocks to close friendship, but each one can be combated by the positive side of the same trait.

Celebration Instead of Exclusion

Most cartoonish depictions of female friendship emphasize one thing: cliquishness. The story has been told again and again of the pink princess and her cohort of snobs who have divided the school into neat categories of who is nerdy or cool, in or out. We laugh at these caricatures and critique them, but almost all of us have experienced cliques at some point—and not just within the walls of middle school. As we grow older, we encounter the accursed clique everywhere: in grad school, at work, at church. I'm increasingly cognizant that the world is mostly run by well-groomed, professional middle-schoolers.

I saw an article recently (one of those list articles you click through) whose headline was something along the lines of "What Everyone Hates to Hear about in the Workplace." The first point was something like "Your personal frustrations." *Ah, yes. I suppose that makes sense*, I thought. And then it continued, "Your religious convictions, your family, your political convictions, your leisure activities." On it went, describing in sneering prose how disgusting it would be to hear about anything that might indicate that you are a distinct individual with a history rather than a nameless corporate bondswoman. I laughed incredulously. I am a strong proponent of professionalism, good boundaries, and discretion. But surely the appropriate workplace banter could extend beyond "Gee! What interesting weather we're having. How about those stocks?" This pressure to create an environment void of individuality, where everyone talks the same and looks the same, is the adult equivalent of the Queens at my middle school.

Cliques are binding things, and they give their members an identity. Whether it is the "Plastics" in *Mean Girls* or the drama club or the sanitized workplace imagined in that article, cliques offer the same promise: belonging and identity. *These are my people, and I belong*. The desire to belong and be known is powerful and good. The trouble comes in the way cliques promise to supply these needs: by suppressing the parts of individuals that might threaten the pack. People who are able and willing to do what the group requires to fit in are accepted, while those who cannot or will not hide their incongruities are not to be admitted. Those incongruities could be anything: being too quiet, too loud, too plain, too pretty, too smart, too ordinary, too talented, too skeptical, too religious, too little, too much.

If the price of membership in a group is the muzzling of your personality, the impediment of your growth, the obstruction of your curiosities and passions, or the concealment of your pain, the price is too high. Cliques require this payment because they are weak, being based in nothing more than a mutual fear of being alone, left out, or unimportant. Difference threatens and can break a clique.

The price of true group friendships is consideration of others, kindness, and self-control. The kind of belonging that enables you to grow is the one that makes space for you in your fullness and allows you to make space for others. This is a more sturdy kind of belonging, not dependent on the conformity of all its parts. But it requires a different attitude: celebration.

First, we must learn to celebrate people as the distinctive works of art they are. First John 4:12 says, "No one has ever seen God. But if we love each other, God lives in us, and his love is brought to full expression in us." Or, as Jean Valjean poetically sings in *Les Miserables*, "To love another person is to see the face of God." When I regard the wondrous and sometimes shocking differences I encounter in my friends, I like to think that I am, in some way, encountering a side of God I have never encountered before. For example, I have a friend named Laila who studied sustainable development. When she was not in a lab studying graphs and statistics, she was running along the beach or working in the garden she planted for our dorm. I hate math, I have asthma-scarred lungs (and am also remarkably lazy when it comes to physical exertion), and I have a green thumb but a poor memory, meaning my plants often die of thirst, bless them. Our differences did not shut the door to relationship; they opened the window to discovery. She showed me how intricate, mathematical, sturdy, and yet delicate our planet is. In her I saw a care for detail, a precise nurturing, and a quiet faithfulness that I still appreciate these years hence. She saw the world differently from the way I see it, and I am richer for it.

Second, we must learn to celebrate life—its burdens and

successes. Friendships must be *about* something, meaning we are bonded together through a sense of shared purpose, of joined struggle. My tribe bonded around the business of life—marking endings, beginnings, holidays, accomplishments, and even sorrows together. Celebrations provide a literal space to draw people together. As we stood together in celebration of our little victories, we were bonded by more than our fear; we were bonded by joy. Nothing can bond people more than food and celebration. And no one is better at weaving the magic of a joyful celebration than the women I know.

Encouragement Instead of Jealousy

Nothing kills the bonds of trust and goodwill like comparison and jealousy. A mentor of mine used to say that the results of comparison will always damage you. Either you will feel better than others and become prideful, or you will feel inadequate, embarrassed, and dissatisfied with yourself. When you start comparing yourself to people, you begin to set them in competition with yourself. You begin seeing people as opponents to beat, not friends to love.

Competition is based in a mind-set of scarcity—the idea that there is not enough approval to go around. If I think of you as my competitor, your beauty, intelligence, or magnetism becomes a threat to my own identity. But it is so difficult not to compare! In my experience, nowhere is this more difficult to wrestle with than in academia, where every mark on a paper or nod of approval from a professor could mean an acceptance, a scholarship, a publishing agreement. But comparison is pervasive in every stage of life; we compare our looks, our love lives, our jobs, our intellect, our success, our spiritual prowess.

For too long, women have been pitted against each other, as though there is room for only one successful woman or one beautiful woman or one woman with a happy marriage. Comparison eviscerates our ability to truly care for others, because as long as we are invested in determining whether someone else's success or sorrow makes us feel better or worse about ourselves, it is impossible for us to care about the good of the other person. In competition there are winners and losers; there are no companions.

I am grateful that throughout my life, I have had friends who are exceptions to this comparison trap. My truest friends are not competitors, they are encouragers.

Encouragement has sometimes been sentimentalized, made to sound fluffy and unimportant. But it is neither of these things. The core of the word is *courage*, which is "the ability to do something that frightens one; bravery" or "strength in the face of pain or grief." To encourage someone is to push her towards courage, to call her to courage, to help her be courageous. When we compete with each other, we hope others will trip and fall in the race of life. When we encourage each other, however, we spur one another to bravery, to excellence, to victory.

Life requires so much courage. In the last year alone, my friends have gotten married, broken up with their boyfriends, finished master's degrees, had miscarriages, gotten into PhD programs, moved, battled illness, grieved over lost loved ones, and celebrated the arrival of new life. Life is too much to take on alone, but it is far too much when burdened with the weight of competition. Rather than seeing one another as competitors, threatening each other's success, we must learn to see one another as coconspirators in bringing life and light to the world. A group of friends should be a team of advocates, fighting fiercely for one another's victories, weeping at their setbacks, cheering as they run and run well, and crying with pride and delight when they cross the finish line.

To center our relationships on courage instead of competition requires a conscious decision of the heart. That was a decision I was reminded of in my time with the Tribe. There were two months during my master's that felt like a boxing match. Each day seemed to hold another knock, another disappointment. I felt concussed and confused. At the same time, Macie's life was looking up; she got into a wonderful program with nearly full funding. I was so tired and downtrodden that I was tempted to let my glumness swallow up my excitement for her. Didn't I deserve to be sad? But her success was not in competition with my sadness. So we celebrated, I forgot about myself for an afternoon (a great relief, honestly!), and we gloried in the marvelous human that she is.

Soon another sorrow came knocking on my door, and it just about knocked me out. Jenna caught me in the throes, let me cry, made me tea, and settled me back in my room. I listened to music and nursed my grief; I was resigned to waiting out the grayness. Then Macie knocked on my door. She had mushroom risotto and chocolate. A word couldn't make it out of my mouth before she hugged me long and tight as I melted into tears.

Those gestures meant more than I can say. It was such a gift that she, in the stride of her hope, would meet me and love me in my moment of heartache. But that is the room that friendship can make. There was room enough for her happiness and for my sorrow. And there was courage enough for both the joy and the grief.

Confrontation Instead of Gossip

"Friendships nowadays can't take the bumps they used to," one of my friends said recently. She studies how the interpersonal relationships of certain famous Scots in the nineteenth century shaped their writings and philosophy. Her subjects maintained close friendships over many years, weathering the strain of distance and disagreement. Many saw their written works as the fruit of such friendships, the outgrowing of many years of engagement and growth. Part of that growth was caused by differences and by wrangling over ideals. To them, she said, a disagreement or a personal tension was not the sign of an imminent end to the relationship but an invitation to deeper confidentiality.

What are such durable alliances made of? My friend had a simple answer: trust. The dictionary defines trust as the "firm belief in the reliability, truth, or ability of someone." We can put our weight on things that are reliable and trust that they will not break. To be able to trust someone, we must know that they are for us and not against us, that they are not going anywhere, and that they will not disappear with all our personal secrets in tow. We must know that they are truthful and genuine, that they will not tell us one thing and then roll their eyes and complain about us behind our backs. The friends my classmate studied had fiery friendships, full of tensions and disagreements, philosophically and personally. Their friendships could withstand these frictions because there was an underlying bond of trust, an assumption that they would move towards unity, if not sameness, in their differences. They could lean on the friendship in troubles, in disagreements, in distance, and they knew it would not break.

Gossip, in contrast, breaks trust. When we gossip, whether it is sharing someone's personal secrets and troubles or spreading our resentment over the actions of another, we rot the foundation of friendship. How can others trust our friendship if we may ruin them without warning? How can others lean on a friendship that isn't strong enough to support their weight? Gossip shows, first of all, that we do not have the other person's best in mind. But it also shows a lack of willingness to engage in healthy confrontation; we would rather vent our frustrations to an outside party who has nothing to do with our friendship troubles than tell our friend what has hurt or offended us. Sometimes we mask our lack of willingness to confront as consideration for the other person's feelings; we wouldn't want to hurt them or cause undue conflict! In my case, this is, more often than not, a desire to preserve my own reputation as a nice person; it isn't really out of consideration for the other person. Complaining is easier. I'd rather whine to an external source and do nothing to bring wholeness to my friendship.

Confrontation can nurture trust and demonstrate love. Proverbs 27:6 says, "Wounds from a sincere friend are better than many kisses from an enemy." The language of this verse is jarring. What is a faithful wound? How could wounding—hurt—ever be faithful? Surgery requires faithful wounds. Surgery, while often scary and almost always inconvenient, does many useful things: it mends something broken or removes a dangerous growth. Most of us, at some point in our lives, require surgery. Surgery heals, but it requires an incision, a cut, a wound. It opens something that needs to be opened and closes something that needs to be closed. To avoid the faithful wound of surgery is foolish, blind, and sometimes downright self-sabotaging.

The faithful wounds of a friend are like surgery; they seek to mend and to heal. To confront a hurt or frustration in a friendship is to say, "I care enough about you and about this friendship to not let quiet resentment grow like a cancer in my heart." Paradoxical as it may sound, I have found that confrontations, including when I'm being confronted myself, have often brought me closer in friendship and even made me feel loved.

Gossip is a wound, but it is not faithful. In contrast, confrontation done in love and humility and hope is a faithful wound that leads to health, growth, and trust.

I still live in St. Andrews, but the rest of the Tribe does not. I miss them terribly. I do not think the closeness of life and friendship I found with them will be easily, if ever, repeated. But even as I miss them, I am thankful. It is good to have something so worth grieving.

If you have experienced the goodness of your own Tribe, you know the sweetness and strength that I've tried to capture in these pages. And if you've only experienced pain or dissatisfaction from shallow and harmful groups of people, I understand, and I pray for you to find the net of support and delight that your heart longs for.

When friendships like these do arise, embrace them and do what you can to treasure and keep them, even if you live at a distance. Because there is nothing like the celebration, the encouragement, and the faithful wounds of a tribe of excellent women.

CHAPTER 10

The Hospitable Friend

*Hospitality is not to change people, but to offer
them space where change can take place.*

HENRI NOUWEN

SALLY ℘ "Chilled to the bone" had new meaning to us as
we huddled together, scampering along the cobbled road under
too-small umbrellas while being pelted with sideways-blowing
rain. Earlier that morning, as we left our bed-and-breakfast, our
English hostess had proclaimed, "You're in for a wet day today.
Wear your jumpers [sweaters] and wellies [rubber boots, English
style] so you don't get drenched, as it will be pouring all day."

Having no wellies and only American-style raincoats, we ven-
tured into the heavy drizzle with adventuresome hearts. Our
umbrellas frequently flew inside out in the brisk wind, which
meant we were just holding sticks that offered no protection. Pools

of water companioned our steps and soaked our socks and shoes as we plodded on our course.

Our destination was a small passenger boat, tied up and tossing wildly on the shore of a lake. Boarding the boat was daunting amid the mess of the stormy wetness, but the captain of the little ship was not intimidated in the least by the menacing waves. So we tentatively stepped into the soaked boat and tried desperately not to fall into the water that was gathering on the floor.

The four of us giggled and chattered and wiped our faces and wet eyelashes and marveled at the adventure on which we found ourselves. This was the trip we had been planning and dreaming about for years—a Girls' Club adventure to England with thirteen-year-old Joy, twenty-four-year-old Sarah, and my seventy-two-year-old cherished friend Phyllis—three of my kindred spirits and closest of friends. Our mission was to visit the homes of many of our favorite English authors whose great literature had stirred our souls. Dickens, Shakespeare, Wordsworth, Beatrix Potter, and James Herriot were some of the authors whose homes we would tour on our eight-day adventure. We decided to save Tolkien and Lewis for a future trip.

The reality of seeing our dream come true added to our sense of accomplishment and deep mutual pleasure as we followed our well-planned journey. We had all saved for months, used travel points, and studied each location we would visit. Somehow, as we had dreamed of this day, it did not involve a flooding storm in the midst of our tour.

True, the stormy sea added to our excitement and the story we were living together in that moment, but we were thrilled and relieved to disembark after twenty minutes of bouncing and tipping upon the dark, tossing waves.

"Walk up the path on the side of the road, and you will see the way to her house," the boatman directed.

On the way, we encountered more rain, more wind, and more muddy sloshing, but joy still fluttered in our hearts in our mutual story. This was a great crew of women, all hearty and determined to enjoy the day, no matter the circumstances. It is always a blessing to travel with uncomplaining companions, as it keeps everyone going forward and determined to enjoy the days.

Finally, after stumbling through the perfect little garden where Peter Rabbit must have played and rolled in muddiness, we took mincing strides towards the front of the house and into the door of the tiny cottage, where we found refuge from the wetness. Finally, we had arrived at the quintessentially charming Hill Top, the famous home of Beatrix Potter.

A fire was roaring in the grate of the tiny fireplace, and as we began to take in the room, we felt confident our journey was being rewarded according to our great expectations. *Charming* took on new meaning for us in her modest little home. Dark, elegant hand-carved pieces of furniture graced each wall and corner—a chair here, a hutch there, and a lovely little settee and welcoming table in the dining room. As we shivered and made our way through the house, we knew Beatrix Potter had been a kindred spirit. It was evident in the way she loved beauty, chose craftsmanship and color, and filled her home with treasures of her own finding.

Having toured countless historical homes over the years with my children, I think this might be the most delightful and pleasant, warm and inviting place I have ever toured. Potter's personal possessions and notes lay open in all the nooks and crannies as though she were just out on an errand and would pop through the front door at any moment.

Our guide obviously loved telling the author's story. Beatrix Potter was not only a writer; she was also an astute businesswoman and philanthropist. In a time when women were not generally accepted as having a place in the marketplace of publishers, merchandising, and economics, she became one of the most prosperous people in her lifetime. And there we were, stepping through the corridors where she had worked, lived, created, and dreamed of the legacy she would leave with her life.

As she cared for her community and her country, Potter started buying up farms around her home to preserve the land from being overdeveloped by those who wanted to ravage it for commercial use. By the time she died, she had bought fourteen farms and four thousand acres of land and donated it to the British National Trust, ensuring that the area would be preserved in its raw beauty, never to be sold or used for commercial projects. Consequently, the Lake District where she lived has become a haven for hikers, naturalists, and those who want a place to get away from the busyness of city life.

Before we began our trip, we did not know that this author would become a mentor to us in the ways of living into our potential. But all of us left her home with a fire in our hearts to live into our own callings. We had been in the presence of someone whose legacy inspired our own. One of the best gifts a friend can give is to create space to allow inspiration and dreaming to become a part of the atmosphere. In doing so, we call each other to be our best selves, to live into our potential.

Now that we'd finished our inspection of all the nooks and crannies of Potter's delightful cottage, we knew we had to brave the cold and wet weather one more time. Steaming, strong English tea was calling our names to cheer us along our way. However, when we arrived at the local teahouse, we discovered that it was closed that day. So we headed for a tiny white stucco pub that had wispy, curling smoke dancing out of the old chimney, promising warmth inside its walls.

A tiny, rough wooden table, situated against the streaming windowpane overlooking the pathway where we had just tromped, was free for the taking. In that moment, the four of us kindred spirits huddled close with an affection and joy that bound our hearts—and, at that moment, our bodies—together.

As we filled the small room with twitters of laughter and the camaraderie of our mutual adventure, our hearts were knit even closer together. We shared our soulish thoughts, our dreams, and our hopes around steaming cups of tea that warmed our hands and our hearts.

"Beatrix was a writer just like you girls," commented Phyllis. "I would love to hear about the stories you would like to write, the books you might try to publish, and how her life inspired you to leave your mark on the world." She thoughtfully started with Joy, the youngest. "Joy, you go first. You always have the most interesting things to say. Did you notice the many ways she left a legacy? How does that speak to us of what we might do if we lived as intentionally and confidently as she did in her own arena?"

I watched my friend verbally affirm my girls, caressing their hearts with words that said, *Your life has possibility. I believe in you. I am interested in you.*

The gift of showing such intentional attention by crafting words directed at their hearts is something long practiced by this woman who has invested her whole life in mentoring others. And as she mentored my own girls, I soaked up her example in my heart, learning to artfully ask questions of others to draw them out.

This was the grid Phyllis has carried in her relationship with my family and with others throughout the years: "How can I affirm, draw out, encourage, and show love and affection to those God brings across my path?"

Her heart is committed to the essence of hospitality—caring for us, her friends, no matter where we share the moment. Her hosting of us is not dependent on place but on the way she takes care of our friendship wherever we find ourselves. True hospitality emerges in real life from a heart that is ready to give and to serve. The way one serves and cares follows a heart commitment.

The girls looked thoughtfully into their cups amid long, full sips of the dark brew and then began to open a window into their own dreams. We all still remember the conversation Phyllis's questions engendered. How fun, ten years later, to see that the girls have actually followed the dreams they shared about that day. Through lots of hard work and perseverance, both have become published authors. Perhaps the flame to become writers was kindled in that very conversation.

This momentous occasion, unnoticed by the outer world, called for a photograph, a way to capture the memory and significance of this personally treasured occasion. In the picture, each of us is grasping a white porcelain cup of tea while spontaneously placing our hands together in a tight circle—an unconscious gesture of toasting and a commemoration of this sacred time in our friendship. The precious, delicate hands of Sarah, my beloved first child, are on the left. The lovely, gently weathered hands of my cherished friend Phyllis, who has mentored all three of us, are next to Sarah's. The darling, soft little hands of my truly "joy-full" youngest daughter, Joy, on my right, join with my own hands, which clasp hers and Sarah's on the other side. A large teapot in the middle signals the importance of our teatime commitments, both in ordinary moments and on special occasions like that one. I have cherished this beloved picture ever since it was taken.

To me this picture reflects true hospitality—the joy of love shared, memories made, and fellowship embraced. At its most basic level, hospitality means looking to meet one another's needs: welcoming one another, intently looking for opportunities to affirm one another, carrying heavy bags, sharing the last piece of fruit, rubbing weary feet, offering a shoulder to nap on in a swaying train. With each moment that we clustered together, we were learning the secret of taking care of one another, of whispering worth to each person's heart. Hospitality starts with initiative, an invitation, a phone call, a meal offered.

Learning to Focus

Recently I have been pondering the story of Jesus' visit to Mary and Martha's home. Luke 10:38-42 is such a short story, but it is amazingly poignant in the truth it holds. While Jesus was visiting, Mary came to sit near Him, to be present and attentive to Him in relationship. Martha kept up her preparations so the details could be "just right." But Jesus rebuked Martha, saying, "My dear Martha, you are worried and upset over all these details! There is only one thing worth being concerned about. Mary has discovered it, and it will not be taken away from her."

I have been looking at this passage from the point of view of friendship. We are often so busy and distracted by life and duties that we relate halfheartedly to our husbands, our children, and our friends. We look at our cell phones, check social media, and rush around while "sort of listening" to what is being said. Even when we invite others to our homes or meet at a coffee shop, we can easily be distracted from looking into the heart of the person sitting right in front of us. Have we gotten out of the habit of dropping everything in order to focus on the face, the eyes, the needs, and the words of our friends and children?

I think Mary is a picture to us of the real heart of hospitality in friendship. Our friends do not feel our love when we are distracted by other tasks. At its heart, hospitality means learning to focus on the people God brings our way by really listening to their words and looking to see what their faces, expressions, and hearts are communicating. I think this story gives us deep insight into friendship and hospitality. The friendship between Jesus and Mary grew because Mary was focused on this amazing opportunity to be close to Him. Martha was distracted and unfocused, so she missed out on being affirmed by her dearest and most cherished Friend.

When I am focused on my task at hand instead of on the preciousness of a relationship, I am in danger of missing an intimate moment with my loved one. Blessed friendship progresses through focused time and attention—through offering others our best attentiveness when we are together.

Helping Others Live into Their Potential

When I think of my purpose in crafting my blog several years ago, it was this scene from our blustery day in England that was on my heart and taking shape in my mind. Since there is rarely friendship or companionship like that of spiritually strong women celebrating life and cultivating love together, I wanted my blog to be a place of hospitality to the women who joined me there. My desire was and is that they would find a warm welcome, a message of "I understand you and am walking a similar journey to the one you're on." I want to be an encouragement to women, because each life matters. The same is true of my books and podcasts— I long for them to be a place of camaraderie and mutual kinship. I want to give women a glimpse of my home, beautiful and messy, with a dog, phone calls, crumbs in the corner, and the possibility of living a great life in the middle of such details.

I have been blessed to have collected spiritually alive, generously loving companions and the dearest of friends throughout my life, and this is what has strengthened me to continue on my pathway of ideals—finding light and beauty, and cultivating all that is good and godly in the ordinary moments of life.

Jesus made a habit of gathering people around Himself, and then He generously poured out His life to them. And so, as women of faith who seek to gather all that is good, true, and beautiful, we see life growing and spawning new life as a result of being together, with Him in our midst. The joy of being known and invited in is best shared around mutually held values and beliefs. In this context, we gather with like-minded friends who long for that personal touch of love and the true fellowship of sharing together in the reality of walking with Him amid the warp and woof of our lives. We share in the joy that can come only from Him, our best and dearest companion, who lives fully in our midst.

I see times like this as necessary for my soul, so that when I am weary or discouraged, I can find His water of life flowing on my dry soul through the precious friends who refresh me.

That moment when the four of us were drinking tea was not the first time I'd seen Phyllis's hospitality in action. By that point

Phyllis and I had already been meeting together for years, helping each other through dark passages, encouraging one another in our walk with the Lord, and mutually initiating friendship. She has been a real, in-the-flesh picture of hospitality to me, and she calls me to live into my own potential of welcoming other people God brings to me.

I have never been as good a friend to Phyllis as she has been to me. I do not deserve and have never earned her attention, her generosity to me, her love. And yet because she is willing to give more than I do, I have been able to persevere in my extremely demanding ministry to the outside world as well as keep my priorities straight at home. My online ministry, book deadlines, travels to conferences, and attention to the constant needs of my family have meant that I have to keep boundaries and personal limits on what I can reasonably give to others. Yet Phyllis seems to understand my limitations, my drifting towards exhaustion from time to time. It is as though she has taken it upon herself to be my angel-supporter, because that is the essence of who she is for everyone she meets. She never seems to notice that she is usually the initiator, the one who cares for me. I think God saw that I was living a constantly draining life, and He gave me the gift of Phyllis to keep me going when I wasn't even aware of what I needed.

I remember countless times breathing in the grace I received in her home. The biggest grace to me has been that even when I am overwhelmingly busy with book deadlines, marketing, speaking engagements, book launches, blog posts, podcasts, and of course the constant and heavy demands of my family, she understands. She looks into my life and chooses to be committed even when I cannot be available.

Phyllis has had many roles over the years: she was on staff with

Navigators, ran a business out of her home, teaches yearly discipleship groups, and hosts her four children and many grandchildren on a regular basis. She has very little time to spare in a demanding schedule. Yet somehow she makes me a priority. I don't know how she manages it. But sometimes God calls us to be friends with those who give to us even when we do not have the resources to give back. I learned that gift firsthand from her.

I have never felt judged, criticized, or manipulated by Phyllis. She knows that I can be judgmental of others at times, and that I can be critical because of my own tower of ideals. Yet she loves me and models what mature, unconditional love looks like, without lecturing me for my selfish focus. I count on her for wisdom because she is older and more experienced in almost all areas of life than I am. I just know that I might not have made it through the demands of my life without her constantly seeking me out. Phyllis has always been my devoted, truly hospitable friend.

Becoming a "Friend Hospital"

Hospitality has the same basic root and meaning as the words *hospital*, *hospice*, and *hotel*. At its best, hospitality speaks of a person who hosts and serves others, with their well-being, health, and welfare at heart and the meeting of their needs planned out. Hospitality comes from an attitude that says, "I am willing to give of myself to meet your needs so that you feel supported, loved, cared for, served, and inspired." Phyllis was so often my hospital—a place where I was safe, warm, and cared for.

As I search the landscape of my life, there are years and years in which I taught Bible studies, hosted meals in my home, wrote countless books and blogs, and spoke at hundreds of conferences.

Often I would become worn out and frazzled from meeting so many personal needs, including those of my family, with very few support systems. A part of my own life story is that I did not have family support systems or babysitters through many of the years my children were growing up.

Phyllis and I never spoke of her being the one who would carry me through these many years of ministry, yet as I look back, she has been there for me, listening, blessing, loving, encouraging, providing, cooking, and giving generous love and attention to me and to my girls. The strengthening, sympathy, and spiritual foundation I needed to be able to accomplish what God had for me to do came through His provision of Phyllis.

I didn't even know I needed her when we first met, but I believe that she has been an angel-gift from God to keep me from faltering. I have seen that God cares about my having friends, even when this was something I didn't know to pray for.

From the earliest times of meeting with Phyllis, I drank water for my thirsty heart, soul, and body. She always prepared her home and every aspect of her life to extend the love, beauty, words, and purposes of Christ to all who entered. Her home was a place dedicated to bringing Christ alive, whatever the need of the person who came her way. I knew that if I took time to be with her, I would always be drawing from the well of spirituality in which she invested daily. I would leave her presence wanting to love God more, full of determination to be more faithful and excited to live more purposefully.

Whenever I entered Phyllis's home, the candles would already be lit, and cookies, a fresh salad, or small tidbits of fruit, cheese, and nuts would be on the table where we would meet. Sometimes we would sit in front of the cozy fireplace in her den; other times we would meet in her tearoom, with books and music surrounding us. My favorite times were when we met outside on her deck, where containers of flowers would be blooming wildly and we had a view of the Colorado mountainside, with aspen trees shimmering through soft breezes and wildflowers singing a song over our time together.

Hospitality was something Phyllis started investing in long before anyone entered her home. She made a commitment to serve others the way Christ served. Jesus washed His friends' feet, fed His disciples with both real food and spiritual food, embraced outcasts, and touched those who were in need. And so Phyllis became for me an incarnational source of the love, encouragement, and messages of God.

Depression has attacked me from time to time over the years— those dark feelings that suggest that I am inadequate, that my sin will exclude me from being used by God, that I cannot keep going. Whether as a result of the demands and "drainings" of my husband, my children, or the women I minister to, I have sometimes felt that I was going under. My tendency to give out more than I take in takes its toll at times. When I need wisdom about how to proceed or when I am plagued by a strong desire to quit, I know I need to reach out for help. I have learned that when I feel this way, I need to ask Phyllis to meet with me because she will help carry me and lift me above my heavy load.

I must add, too, that there are many people in my life who started out as strangers and eventually became dear friends because I invited them into my home. Often when we establish a loving, accepting atmosphere and offer an invitation, we find people are ready to share their hearts, their needs, their dreams, their fears, and their hopes. A heart that says "Welcome" will find a variety of people responding to friendship.

The Marks of a Hospitable Friend

Phyllis has inspired me with her strength. I know I can always draw life from her, and I want to become that kind of person for others too—especially my friends and my daughters. As I think about it, there are several traits Phyllis exhibits that make her such a good friend. I've adopted these in my own life in my attempt to grow as a friend.

1. BECOME A GO-TO FRIEND.

Determine to be the one who will be there *no matter what*. Practice being faithful and uncritical, choose to give grace, adopt a heart of thankfulness for all the times you have been blessed by your friend, and determine to be consistently loyal. Make a commitment that says, "I will be there for you regardless of the season, even when we disagree, no matter the circumstances of life. I will do this because I believe God has called me to be your committed friend." A go-to friend calls and initiates because it is the right thing to do, not because it's her turn. We must carefully choose who we will be this kind of friend for; we cannot be this committed with many people. But with the people we are committed to, we should be faithful and consistent. So many times when I was snowed under with life, Phyllis called me, invited me to her home, prayed for me, and sent me encouraging texts. She knew I needed her, so she gave out of the goodness of her heart.

2. COMMIT TO MEETING YOUR FRIEND'S NEEDS.

Just as a hospital offers the precise treatment a patient needs, learn to tend to the needs, desires, and aches of your friends. Practice being someone who is available to help, pray, encourage, and lift up your friend at any time, no matter what. Deciding to become that kind of friend takes a decision on your part, and it will test you at times. But this type of long-term promise will also build your own integrity. A number of years ago, I asked Phyllis if she would meet with me every week that she was in town and I was in town, and we have done so ever since. Recently another friend, Beth, said to me, "Rarely does anyone reach out to me, and yet, because of my love for Jesus, I keep initiating and reaching out to friends. That is what He modeled for me to do." We need to reach out and provide a haven of rest and encouragement for others. When we do, we are giving others a taste of the hospitality of Christ. If we follow Him, we will always be giving more than we are receiving. As we mature, it will be our joy to serve with unmixed motives, just for the love of it.

3. SEEK TO BE A WISE FRIEND.

Every time I see Phyllis, she has a new thought or insight that she is ready to share with me. When I am with her, I learn and grow, and I am drawn closer to God. Proverbs 13:20 says, "Walk with the wise and become wise." I have had to be intentional about looking for these kinds of friends over the years. I once heard a leader say, "I will go to the ends of the earth to be around someone who makes me want to love God more and be more excellent. I will run fast away from the kind of person who is always a drain—someone who complains, drags me down, and depletes my desire to walk with God." I have thought a lot about this philosophy over the years. We must all minister to a wide variety of people, yet when it comes to seeking out friends to spend time with, I have purposefully looked for women who have the life of Christ bubbling up inside them. These friends fill my own heart with wisdom and keep me pursuing God and His holiness.

Positive peer pressure, you might say. Phyllis makes me want to love God more.

I read an article once that said if you don't want to be lonely and you want friends when you are in your seventies, pick your closest friends and set aside a planned time each year when you will spend quality time together. I chose eight such friends (a group that includes Sarah and Joy). For the past two years, I have planned times when I can be with these friends to celebrate life, share what is on our hearts, and make new memories. I want to build on these friendships every year for my remaining years. If we don't give friendships priority time, prepared and planned in advance, we will find ourselves lonely one day.

Wise, excellent women are hard to come by, yet when I have found them, they are dedicated to pursuing God no matter what. Their priorities show the investment they have made in spending time with the Lord on a regular basis and then walking obediently, choosing to serve Him and His ways. These women are not perfect, and many of them have difficult and scarred backgrounds, having learned Scripture and truth by pursuing it. But as they have pursued the Lord and obeyed His Word, they have become reflections of Christ. When I meet someone who is "forgetting what lies behind" (Philippians 3:13, ESV) and is pursuing wisdom, faith, and a love for God, we have fellowship, whatever the differences in our age or experience.

How about you? Are you a wise friend? Are you investing in wisdom by reading books that lead you to more insight into life? Are you seeking to study and understand the Word of God? Are you growing in the direction of maturity and making the hard choices to build a legacy of faith and faithfulness? Are you a giver in reaching out to others and seeking to offer love to the brokenhearted? If so, you will be a friend who offers wisdom, compassion, comfort, and insight to those in your inner circle.

4. STORE FAITH, TRUTH, AND INTEGRITY IN YOUR OWN LIFE.

Galatians 6:7 says, "Whatever one sows, that will he also reap" (ESV). When we sow good things in our lives, we aren't the only ones who benefit—our friends do too. Phyllis has sown prayer, love, wisdom, and thoughtfulness, and every time I am with her, I reap the good consequences. Her example has filled me with a desire to be a source of spiritual truth to my friends.

Do you want your children, friends, neighbors, and husband to draw from the life that is bubbling over from your heart and mind and words and attitudes? Then you must spend day after day with the Word of Life, who will give you the true wisdom you long for. Determine that you will read the Bible every day. Choose to believe in God every day, in every circumstance, because that is the way to please Him. Pray for His guidance, and live with His presence beside you. It is the engaged, loving heart—the one that hungers to know and live for God—that will become the heart others will draw from. No cleverness or self-strength or rules or formula can replace the palpable life that comes from living day by day holding on to God's hand and then being a wellspring from which others can draw.

Even as a house is built one brick at a time and yet has the potential to become a mansion, so a wise woman builds her house one day, one brick, at a time until it has a strong spiritual foundation. Your friends will draw from what you have been sowing, so be sure you are sowing what you want them to reap.

I am thankful for every friend who has stored goodness in her heart and has given generously to me in friendship, because these have helped me to keep going in my own life of faith. I treasure each of them. I am especially thankful for Phyllis, for all the time she has spent with God so that I could be with Him when I am with her. But even more, I hope that I am a Phyllis to other people, because I recognize how important it is for them to have someone who is committed to meeting their needs when life gets overwhelming.

CHAPTER 11

Becoming a Queen

Blessed is the influence of one true,
loving human soul on another.

GEORGE ELIOT

SARAH 〃 There are all sorts of queens in the world, if
only you have the eye to spot them, and I met one my first week
in Oxford. I didn't know it at first; she was an English woman of
quiet cordiality, with a kind, calm presence that I liked but didn't
yet know to respect. She was a tutor at my college, and I first
encountered her early one Tuesday morning when she hosted the
weekly fellowship groups to which every student at my college was
assigned so we could get to know one another on a more personal
level.

That first bright autumn day, with ten or so of us from vastly
different worlds and walks of life gathered in a slightly awkward

silence, she sat in the quiet, smiling at us, unperturbed by the embarrassed or shy glances. I can still remember the quality of our nervous hush, the sense that we were all strangers, and the way she enfolded us with a few words of welcome, a bit of laughter, transforming our meeting into a space of ease and invitation as she drew each of us in turn to say a few words about the adventure that had led us to the study of theology. Somehow her gentle presence and quiet authority began, even that morning, to knit us into a community where we could learn about one another . . . and ourselves.

This, I was soon to discover, was a pattern with Liz, for people grew and came to greater life when they entered her sphere of influence. Her leadership was subtle; we didn't always know it was happening. Her authority was not the front-and-center sort, drawing all eyes to the person in charge. Rather, she exercised her power by creating an atmosphere of possibility, of space, of listening and prayer that her students were invited to enter, where room was made for even the shiest among us to express ourselves and find our place in the larger group. The second week, she asked for a number of us to volunteer to take a week to lead the group. When few hands were raised in response, she went on, "Lead us in a study or an experience of something you love. Show us the music or adventures or abstract mathematics that fascinate you." Overwhelmed by essay deadlines and still feeling a little shy, I held back, but later that day Liz stopped me to say how much she'd enjoyed hearing about the part children's books and literature had played in leading me to the study of theology. Would I do a week on poetry or children's picture books, perhaps? It would be such a gift.

Before I knew what had happened, my name was on the list.

Through her prompting and encouragement, I ended up dragging my whole group of fellow amateur theologians through an exercise in reading poetry aloud and, to their surprise, a bit of poetry writing as well. I keenly remember the apprehension I felt in planning that morning, certain that my fellow students would find the exercise frivolous, too imaginative for staid and solid students of theology. My delight was immense when the whole group complied, when people I barely knew read the poems I brought with expression and joy, when one quiet soul later emailed me a sonnet written after our morning together. My confidence leaped over a wall it hadn't been able to climb for months.

In the afterglow of that triumph, I began to realize the graceful power Liz had used to help me to a place of new discovery. As I continued in Liz's fellowship group and presence, I also began to glimpse the source of that rooted and quiet authority as Liz led us to discover her own passion for spiritual formation. A student of the soul, she thought deeply and creatively about the way Christians can be formed to engage more fully with God's love through liturgy and prayer, spiritual discipline, and community. When she took her turn to lead the group, she drew from this deep well of insight, helping us to discover the practices of morning and evening prayer, to spend time studying the lives of Christians before us, and to think together about what we desired in spiritual community. She spoke to us about art and beauty, about the different realms in which we could look for "Christ [at play] in ten thousand places" (as Hopkins puts it in his poem "As Kingfishers Catch Fire"), and she lived this out through the beauty she brought to those in her care. Our once-a-year dinner at her house was rich in candlelight and homemade food, in a home crammed with art and good books. She cut out articles on literature she knew I'd enjoy and left them in my pigeonhole (my college mail slot, in American terms) along with encouraging notes (each with a tiny watercolor on the back). She suggested I find a place to publish a piece I wrote on the Celtic church, and she encouraged me to keep on with my writing even amid my studies.

I spent three years in Liz's pastoral care, and I now count her a very dear friend. Further, I treasure her as a mentor who has profoundly shaped my idea of what I hope to become when I "grow up." As a teacher, a woman, a learner, a theologian, and a leader, Liz is one of those rare women who image to me what womanhood can look like in its full power. Liz is one of the women I call the queens of the world. After many years of faithful investment in friendship and ministry, study and prayer, she has grown into a place of influence where she rules, in her quiet way, by making it a place of invitation, beauty, and transformation for others. When you enter the "court" of Liz's presence, you are sure to encounter a generosity of wisdom and creativity that challenges you in the kindest of ways. Where Liz reigns, good things happen, close friends are made, and souls grow.

That's what I think it means to be a queen in the realm of relationships, and it's what every woman is on a journey to becoming.

When a woman walks in the ways of a Girls' Club kind of friendship—rooting herself in God's love and learning to nourish and cultivate friendships, to be a giver, to create community in barren places—she is developing a very specific identity. She is learning to see herself not only as a woman who has the power to receive love or even just to give it on a personal level, but also as one whose very life and presence are a realm in which love is embodied. Queenship, I think, is the natural outlet and progression of an emotionally healthy, developing woman as she walks in the company of other women and roots herself in the love of God.

We Clarkson girls take a certain pride in being strong women. This is our idea of queenship: we love owning our identity as women who embrace the capacity to influence the world around us. We are aware that the choices of love and faithfulness give us a certain power, and we love the knowledge that we can use this power to bring the world and the people we love to fuller life. Now, I know that term *power* brings up all sorts of debates in our world; it's often a bit of a dirty word in our society. We tend to think of power or authority as questionable or inherently abusive, or at the very least inescapably self-serving. The idea of queenship may initially seem off-putting—am I suggesting that women develop a superiority complex in order to boss people around?

Not at all. The power of queenship as I understand it is rooted in self-giving. Power, in my terms, means that the more love you have received, the more grace you have known, and the more beauty you have experienced, the more capacity you have to be a giver. To be a strong, queenly woman means to pour yourself out for others. To be queenly, at heart, is to daily image God, who used His power to offer the gift of Himself in Christ.

This is the kind of womanhood to which the Girls' Club draws us. It's what I believe God created us to attain, and I strongly believe that the authority and power it gives us are ideals we are called to pursue. The world needs women who have the hearts of queens. We live in a world of lost, confused people, of lonely children, of people who have never known truth or belonging. When we, as women, grow strong through the gift of friendship, through the practice of love, we are called to use our strength to serve and heal those who suffer and grieve.

Love is a huge and marvelous stewardship. Love challenges us to act, to extend the grace we've received to those who are grieved and alone, to use our power to turn one corner of the fallen world into a place where beauty reigns, where people can "taste and see" the goodness of the Lord (Psalm 34:8). This is the kind of queenliness I've seen in my mom and reached for with my sister as we challenge each other to excellence and delight in each other's capacity. Queenship is the natural outcome of our friendship, the natural ripening of love as it makes us strong to give in our turn. And queenship is an identity waiting for every woman.

I have been formed by queenly women throughout my life. They come in countless forms, and each queen I have known looks different, because each woman reflects a different facet of God's life, embodies a different shade of His color and goodness. Some queens I've known are leaders; others are quiet creators. Some are hosts, and some are teachers, but all are women who live with intention and care, who embrace their capacity to shape the world, whose lives are an embodiment of love. Each of these women has personally taught me, in her own way, that women have the power to creatively and dynamically shape the worlds of their home and ministry, their work and community. They have the power to invite, to teach, to correct, to comfort. They have the capacity to help people change or offer them the refuge they need in order to grow. They are able to learn, understand, and teach. Each of those women also taught me that I, too, am called to grow into the same kind of gracious capacity, and they set me on the road to maturity by their mentorship and investment in my story.

What I hope to pass along here is a little of what they taught me.

When I consider what it means to be a leader and a servant, one who rules her corner of the world with grace, a gallery of great women comes to mind. I've encountered them in real life and in story, but each "portrait" in my gallery embodies a certain character quality that I have come to believe is integral to what Joy and I laughingly call "full-bodied, full-blooded" womanhood, the sort that changes just a bit of the fallen world. These qualities include confidence and compassion, wisdom and generosity, endurance and joy. In the section that follows, we'll look at a few of these traits in depth through three lenses: the story of a woman who embodied them (who), an exploration of what that quality is in its richness (what), and how that quality can be sought and cultivated in us as we grow towards that fullness of love that makes queenship of our lives as well (how).

Confidence

Who: Jean and Jenni

The first time I visited England, I was a shy and idealistic twenty-one-year-old who had hopped the great pond of the Atlantic to attend my first intellectual conference in Oxford. At that moment in my story, I was searching for my place in the world. It would be literally a decade before I discovered my vocation in full—ironically, in a small Oxford college where I came to study theology—but I couldn't have known that at the time. What I did know, the first day of the conference, was that I had just been given a glimpse of something I hoped to become. I saw it in a kind, lovely, brisk old woman in a neat suit who rose to give a compelling talk on ethics in the postmodern world. Her name was Jean Bethke Elshtain; she was an ethicist and a professor, a woman of great learning, and moreover, an image of the confident, articulate, passionate womanhood that I wanted to attain.

She was wondrous to me—this model of grace and intelligence, radiant in her calm conviction as she taught. I watched her, loving the insight she brought to modern life, the way she challenged us to ethical, compassionate, just action in our own corners of society, and I yearned for the confidence she embodied. A thousand young convictions were growing in my heart in that season. I looked at the world around me and saw grieving people and broken relationships, and my mind and soul ached with desire to take part in telling the truths that can heal the world. At that moment of youth and insecurity, I couldn't yet imagine how I would gain the strength to teach so clearly, to speak so boldly, to lead others as she did. But the image of Elshtain in her dignity and strength helped me to hope that someday I would.

What: Unself-conscious Courage

Genuine confidence is a rare and wondrous gem of a trait, but it's something every queenly woman I know possesses. Elshtain had it when speaking to a room full of theologians and students; my mom has it when she speaks at conferences on motherhood and discipleship; I see it in women all around me who create art or start Bible studies or adopt children. They share this quality of fearless assurance that drives them to act in profoundly creative ways. What's curious is that their confidence is largely unself-conscious, a quality that is not based on ego or pride but that grows from a heart so rooted in God's reality, so formed by goodness, that excellent action grows out of it.

Confidence is rooted in truth. Courage comes from conviction. And both of these qualities grow as women engage with the truth and goodness of God as it comes to them in Scripture, in friendship, in prayer, and in the written word. When I saw

Elshtain that day and hungered for her surety, what I had yet to realize was that my own confidence would come through years of reading Scripture, of choosing to be faithful in hard times, of engaging with great authors who challenged my view of the world. What I had yet to learn was that my confidence would grow in tandem with my knowledge; that the more of God's life and love I understood, the more I would be driven to act upon it without thought of others' opinions or my own comfort.

Confidence is a quality that comes when our gaze is turned upon truth rather than ourselves.

How: Spending Time in the Word

When I think of the women whose confident leadership and wisdom have formed me, a common image comes to mind. I have watched every one of them rise early in the morning to sit with Scripture (and coffee) for a time of quiet and prayer. There is simply nothing in the world to replace the heart-making, soul-forming, courage-building nourishment of Scripture. The Bible contains the one true story of the world; it tells us who we are and what we were created to accomplish. It reminds us that we are redeemed and helps us to hope amid the grief we all must suffer in this broken world. The women I know who encounter God's Word on a daily basis are the ones whose confidence is rooted in a truth they have gained bit by bit, every day of their lives. They operate out of the surety they have found in God's presence.

But all of these women share another trait: they are readers. I am convinced that every woman alive was born to be a reader (see my book *Book Girl* if you want to learn more) because we are all made in the image of a thinking, insightful, creative God. Our brains are primed to learn through words; they are our path to knowledge, to wisdom, to influence. Every woman I know who bears that rooted confidence is also a woman who engages with the written word in great novels or biographies, in current events, in poetry or devotionals. She is a thinker, a woman who engages with ideas rather than just receiving them. Her confidence grows out of her long habit of wrestling through difficult questions, seeking truth, and searching for wisdom.

I learned this during my first year in Oxford as I began to grow in my knowledge of the Bible and watched another radiant woman teach Scripture at my college. When I arrived at Oxford, I was struggling with a deep sense of insecurity. After a decade of floundering about in search of vocation, I felt inadequate and underqualified to be studying at a school like this one. I was too shy at first to engage in debates, because I was unsure of my own convictions. But in addition to Liz, my tutor and mentor, I had the grace of learning from Jenni, my professor of Old Testament. Her vim to teach about God's faithfulness, her confidence in answering hard questions, her joy in what she discovered made her someone I wanted to emulate from the first class I took with her. As I learned and as curiosity and passion grew in me, I began to realize what made Jenni and Liz and Jean special, so beautifully confident. They weren't looking at themselves; their eyes were turned towards the truth they had found like treasure throughout years of faithfulness.

And now it's my turn; in just a few months, I will stand where Jenni and my other tutors stood to deliver their lectures, and I will give a theological talk of my own. I'm far from having the confidence and grace I hope to someday embody, but the fear I have always borne of speaking in public or sounding stupid or simply not doing the best job possible is fading. What grows in its place is my sense of conviction as I study, my desire to share with others the beauty I've found. I find that I am confident without even meaning to be.

Generosity

Who: Gwennie

From the time I was a tiny girl, I've known that Gwennie was the queen of gift giving. Gwennie, my mom's old and bosom friend from her missionary days in Vienna, is also my beloved mentor and kindred spirit. She came to visit us each year at Christmas when I was growing up, and when she did, we children could barely wait for the moment when she would set a pile of presents at each of our feet. Gwennie gave marvelous gifts—bits and bobs she'd picked up in her travels, mixed with a few staples she knew we'd love. I remember my deep, grateful sense as a small child that Gwennie was a generous soul. To be in her presence was to be blessed.

That sense only deepened as I grew. Over time the tiny Christmas gifts were replaced with the birthday tea she hosted when I came to visit her in my teens, the books she brought to share with me, the mouthwatering meals of roast and salad or fresh bread she made when I came for a visit, the Scripture verses she jotted down to share with a spiritually curious young adult. To be in Gwennie's presence has always meant to be blessed indeed.

Gwennie is my image of queenly generosity. She's a soul who makes other souls feel rich. She takes all that she has and offers it in love: her little home, her kitchen table, her food, her joy in the small beauties of ordinary life. It makes no difference whether she's operating from a little apartment in Vienna or a cottage in Kentucky or anyplace else in the world; Gwennie offers herself in love to every person who enters her home.

What: Sharing out of the Overflow

Generosity is an exuberant quality, one that forms in women as love brims over the cup of their hearts. Queenly women see life as a gift. They breathe in the beauty of the earth, they spot grace in the small wonders of the ordinary, they see every good thing that comes their way as evidence that a loving God has them in His hands. Generosity is their response, the shape of their lives, as they celebrate God's goodness by sharing it.

How: Recognizing Grace

Simply put, we can be generous by first being thankful. Generosity and humility are closely related because the women who are abundant givers realize how much they have received. A generous heart begins with a heart primed to see God's goodness in even the smallest graces of life. Gwennie may be generous, but one of her loveliest qualities is the fact that she considers herself rich—and she is, in the joy that makes a feast of ordinary life. When I am with Gwen, I become aware of what a splendid thing it is to taste homemade food, to enjoy the setting of a table with a beloved old pattern of plate, to savor the turning of the autumn leaves or the simple tasks of gardening as gifts from our Creator. Gwennie gives without stint because she sees herself as receiving an immense amount of goodness every day.

Joy

Who: My Mom

When I was in my late teens, my family moved to Tennessee. We thought we'd stay forever, but we only stayed two years, and my goodness, those were hard years. We lived deep in the country—beautiful, luscious Tennessee hill country, to be sure—but country with few bookshops or restaurants, churches or friends. Three of us were teenagers at the time, hungry for friendship and activity, desperate for my parents to provide that even as they dealt with their own set of ministry troubles and financial strain. We had been there three months when it all came to a head and there was a day of general family unhappiness. The humidity was high, emotions higher, and when my dad left for his office and the rest of us faced another long, hot, lonely day, a sense of dread settled in my heart.

But my mom wasn't having it. She lit a candle (which fluttered in the air-conditioning), scrambled some eggs, and brewed good mugs of sweet tea for her restless brood. As we ate, our emotions lightened enough to plan a day of marathon-watching our favorite films, with an interlude for chocolate chip cookie making in the afternoon. But the moment that sticks in my mind most is the one when we trooped in to do the dishes. My family is a household of idealists, none of whom feel it is their particular vocation or pleasure to do dishes. My mom rolled her eyes. But then she did something marvelous: she stuck in a Josh Groban CD and told us to dance while we cleaned. The crazy thing is, we actually did. As good ole Josh's golden tenor got going, we twirled around the kitchen, and my mom was the merriest and cutest of us all.

"Isn't life fun?" she panted at the end, when the dishes were done and the music was fading. With my mom, it certainly was.

In that period of life, one of her signature phrases was "I'm going to go down dancing!" By this, she meant she was going to cling to joy, create life, and live in laughter as long as she possibly could. My mom has a Pollyanna heart, one that searches for the beautiful and good in the world, one that receives life as a rich gift from the hand of her Creator. She lives by joy—a queenly, exuberant joy that brings life to all around her.

What: More than Happiness

Joy is the quality that grows in a woman who has learned to root her emotions and her life in the reality of God's daily, sustaining love. It's not just happiness or an emotional high; it's a deep current of radiant belief in the goodness of God. Joy is what comes to women who have learned to sustain themselves by focusing on beauty, by creating pockets of celebration—women who have cultivated the art of taking joy in the smallest of gifts.

Joy is at the heart of the Proverbs 31 woman who laughs at the future, not because it might not be grievous but because there is a real sense in which nothing can threaten what is rich and living within her. She has wrestled with loneliness or grief and found God faithful. She knows that redemption is coming and that truth makes her a little like Gandalf in *The Return of the King*. Though a battle looms and the wizard's face is lined and gray with care, Pippin the hobbit can still see that "under all there was a great joy: a fountain of mirth enough to set a kingdom laughing, were it to gush forth."[1]

How: Knowing the End of the Story

Joy is maintained by knowing the end of the story, and the only way a woman can keep her hold on it is to hold on to the happy ending on the way. I don't mean that we're just supposed to think about heaven and feel happy. A truly joyful woman is able to laugh even though she has "considered all the facts" (as Wendell Berry puts it in his poem "Manifesto: The Mad Farmer Liberation Front"). She has an identity and a sense of blessedness that is rooted in the promises of Scripture rather than in her circumstances—a blessedness that can come only from an immersion in the story of Scripture itself.

A joyful woman glimpses the happy ending, but she also creates it. For joy is kept and cultivated through celebration. To celebrate life, whether in a family feast or a birthday, by keeping family traditions, or just by brewing a pot of tea and munching a chocolate cookie, is to draw eternity into time. We state our belief in the happy ending of redemption that is coming by living out this joy in the present moment. We picture heaven in our corner of the earth by the joy we create and the life we celebrate.

Surrounded by Queenly Women

I feel here like the author of Hebrews, who found that there simply wasn't enough room to list and describe the countless brave souls whose lives embodied the qualities of faith. I know his frustration, because I feel the same way about the queenly women I have known and the qualities they embody. Endurance, wisdom, spunk, creativity—I want to add each of these to the list and tell you the stories of the women who have shown me exactly what these traits look like in action. I've seen qualities like these imaged in the lives of women around the world, in vastly different circumstances, with gifts and insights unique to their own experiences and stories. But all are the same in this way: I've watched their small corners of the earth expand with hope and love under the power of their gracious influence.

My own journey towards a growing queenliness began as I watched these women live their lives with courage, and that's why I wanted to give you a glimpse of their stories here. If you hunger for that queenliness of soul, that capacity to be someone in whose realm friendship begins, the best thing you can do is immerse yourself in the lives and stories of the women who model the kind of grace you want to live. Seek out mentors. Pursue thoughtful conversations. Ask the women you admire what habits they cultivate in order to keep their own souls rich and generous. Read books—I have been profoundly formed and challenged by the biographies of women like Amy Carmichael and George Eliot, while novels like *Middlemarch* (by George Eliot), *Bleak House* (by Charles Dickens), and *Pilgrim's Inn* (by Elizabeth Goudge) have peopled my imagination with women who draw me onwards to excellence.

Where these queenly women—real and imagined—reign, hearts find healing and new stories begin. It is the challenge of queenly action that I want to pass along to you as we near the end of this book. Will you, as you grow in that rooted friendship with God and others, accept the gift and stewardship of leading the world in the ways of love? To be a friend, to cultivate rich and lasting relationships, to wrestle loneliness to the ground and transform it by love, to be loyal, to forgive—these are courageous, queenly actions, deeds that defy the fallenness of the world and help towards its mending. In your choice to love and your courage to create, you have the capacity to draw others from the darkness of loneliness and despair into the feast and grace of love. The Kingdom comes when we claim our small squares of existence and offer them to Christ as the space in which His life and fellowship can grow.

One of my favorite quotes in the world is by George Eliot, drawn from the close of her novel *Middlemarch* as she describes the impact of one woman's life upon the world:

The effect of her being on those around her was incalculably diffusive: for the growing good of the world is partly dependent on unhistoric acts; and that things are not so ill with you and me as they might have been, is half owing to the number who lived faithfully a hidden life.[2]

A pastor friend of mine says he thinks this quote is one of the best descriptions he's ever heard of the daily Christian life. I think it's one of the best I've found of what a queenly woman can create with her life. May the effect of your own being, and mine, on those around us be the kind that furthers the good of the world as we claim our own spheres of daily life as the space in which friendship grows, communities come to life, hearts are healed, and souls are deeply known. May we, in the queenly power of friendship, invite the Kingdom of love to come.

CHAPTER 12

As You Are Going

*This is my commandment: Love each other in the
same way I have loved you. There is no greater love
than to lay down one's life for one's friends. You are
my friends if you do what I command. I no longer
call you slaves, because a master doesn't confide
in his slaves. Now you are my friends.*

JOHN 15:12-15

JOY "You're going to Gwennie's house."

I had begun kitting myself out, choosing my favorite shirts
and my beloved skort (the skirt/shorts combination perfect for
any active seven-year-old), along with my favorite stuffed animal,
ever since I'd heard the news. My mom was going on an important
speaking trip, and I was to stay with Gwennie, her oldest friend
and my honorary auntie.

With my small suitcase in tow, my mama drove me two hours
to the appointed Cracker Barrel in Clarksville, where I was handed
off to Gwennie.

As far as I was concerned, there was no such thing as a world without Gwennie. There was, and still is, a jovial spirit that saturates the air wherever she goes. Some of my earliest memories are of her yearly Christmas visits. She came with a twinkle in her eye and two dozen little presents. Each of us had an assigned wrapping paper to indicate which gifts were ours. They were usually very simple things—a set of pencils, a notebook, a scarf—but they were always packaged individually, which made them feel so special, so luxurious, so extravagant.

It was comforting to stay with Gwennie. But I was still trepidatious. This was my first time staying with her by myself and my first time being away from home for so long—a whole week! I was nervous and somehow sad. I loved home. I hugged my mama, wished her a tearless good-bye, and was expertly tucked and buckled into the back of the car.

From the driver's seat, Gwennie turned to look at me. Her eyes were sparkling as they always were; she had secrets and surprises, as she always did. She wore a pastel oxford-cloth shirt and a lovely pink lipstick. Her frosted, neatly cropped hair framed her round and inviting face, and the Jerusalem cross she always wore seemed to shine in joint thrill for the adventures to come. Gwennie smiled and produced a small biscuit tin.

"For the drive back," she said.

I balanced the tin on my knobby knees and opened it. It contained two sandwiches and two brownies neatly packed in tin foil—the first of many signs that I had been prepared for, I was expected, I would be taken care of.

The brownies were famously known in our family as "Larla's brownies." Larla was Gwennie's mama. Before Gwennie moved back to the States from Austria, we'd visit Larla, and she'd always make fried chicken and brownies. Her brownies were the stuff of legend; the brownie itself was moist and thick, almost grainy, and the icing was dark and delicious and almost as rich as fudge. Larla's mind was growing drowsy with Alzheimer's by then, but all her sweetness remained. To this day, every time I make Larla's brownies in Scotland, I am reminded of heavy, humid Kentucky evenings, and of Larla quietly rocking in her chair.

On the two-hour drive to Gwennie's house, she asked me questions and played me music while I munched on pimento-and-cheese sandwiches, trying to decide if I liked them, and devoured the brownies, in no confusion regarding my feelings about their decadent deliciousness. Finally we arrived at Eben House. When Gwennie moved back to her childhood home to take care of her mama, she brought new life to it. She planted a Japanese maple next to the front door and hyacinths by the covered porch. She painted the rooms in light garden colors. She named the house Eben (which means "stone"), for its warm, bric-a-brac exterior covered in sandstone.

As the biscuit tin foretold, Eben House had been prepared for me.

I had my own bedroom, sharing a wall with Gwennie's so that if I got frightened I could knock on the wall and wake her up. That evening I was served my very favorite meal: pot roast and mashed potatoes, along with creamed corn from Uncle Edward's garden. *Life away from home,* I thought, *is not so bad.*

Gwennie took me everywhere with her. Each day held prosaic adventures that I found thrilling. One day we planted flowers in the front bed. Another day we went to Uncle Edward's, met his innumerable and enthusiastic dogs, and wandered through his impressive garden with hallways of corn towering over me as he told us jokes, the lines of his weather-beaten face drawn into incalculable mirth. One day we visited Gwennie's sick friend, who never got better. One day we went to the appropriately named Dinky Diner, which probably hadn't been redecorated since 1963. We looked at all the old music posters on the walls, and Gwennie told me about Mama Cass and her crooning voice while the waitress gave me a piece of pie for coming all the way from Nashville. One day we went to Hobby Lobby, where I picked out three kinds of paint—one white, one green, and one rose pink—which I used to paint the metal bread box Gwennie had saved for just that purpose. I painted roses on it, and Gwennie let me fill it with treasures—stickers and colored pencils—and promised to keep it until my next visit. One day we went to a Bible study, and I sat with my ankles politely crossed as all the sweet-smelling women drank sweet tea and studied the pungent words of the prophet Jeremiah and prayed like God was listening.

What I liked best about Gwennie was that she treated me like a person. As a child, I hated it when people treated me as a sub-category of human, talking to me in a high and affected voice, with raised eyebrows and exaggerated expressions. Did they realize how ridiculous they looked? Gwennie didn't hold with such foolishness. She took me with her everywhere she went, asked my opinion, and expected me to be able to help in the kitchen and add something interesting to the conversation. I felt that Gwennie thought I was a fascinating individual—and I think she did.

When the week came to an end, Gwennie tucked me once again into her car with another tin of Larla's brownies. I was excited to see my family and to go home, but I was also sad to leave. What a week it had been! And somehow I felt more grown up than before. Not every seven-year-old can claim a whole week away from home. And I had so many new experiences and skills under my belt: planting a garden, making mashed potatoes, painting bread boxes, understanding a deep Southern accent, and gaining a new appreciation for the BBC. I would miss Eben House.

Gwennie looked back at me. "I'll miss you, sweetie," she said, smiling a little sadly. "I can't wait for your next visit."

Her eyes sparkled with the secret knowledge of a coming surprise.

Mentorship: Teaching by Love

Gwennie is one of the people I owe most to in my development as a person. Her life and love have shown me many things, from how to cook a beef roast to how to sprout dogwood branches to the sweetness and depth of Scripture to the art of sitting with a friend in sadness to the deep value of laughter. She is truly one of my dearest mentors. But most of what I have learned from Gwennie has not been in moments that looked like formal mentorship or that seemed like what we so often think of as "ministry." I simply soaked up those lessons through the nourishing joy of her presence. Gwennie's laugh has taught me more about peace than any book I've ever read.

Mentoring is very much in vogue these days. But sometimes I think our imagination regarding what mentorship (or discipleship or whatever you wish to call it) should look like is stunted. For me, the word *mentorship* conjures up images of well-organized church programs, women's conferences, and twelve-step plans. These structured events are good, but they do not necessarily offer the truths that have stuck to my heart in the ups and downs of life. I think this is because formalized mentoring programs treat life like it is a list of principles to be memorized and understood. So if we feel lost or misunderstood or stuck, we search for another book or another conference, thinking maybe it will contain the truth that will unlock our peace.

We are not computers; we cannot download information about God or life by direct transfer. Life is beautiful and barren and impossibly complex. Books and conferences help us think about our lives, but most of life is not thinking about life—it's living through it. Most often, we do not need a book to teach us how to cook or parent or love (and I love books!). We need someone beside us, pointing us in the right direction, guiding our hands, telling us to whip the meringue just a little more. We learn along the way, beside people, through example and companionship. The most powerful wisdom is passed down side by side, through love. We learn to love not because someone tells us about love but because we have been loved. We learn the way I learned from Gwennie—when someone comes alongside us and treats us as interesting individuals worth the effort and capable of the work.

One of my friends in Scotland was, for a long time, a missionary and an aid worker in a country in the Middle East. Her work was almost always with refugees. She told me once how important friendship was in her ministry.

"If you're a refugee family, and six of you are sleeping in one room on the floor, you don't need someone sitting in their clean, well-lit office and dispensing crystalline truths about God or a pamphlet about how to get a job in this country. None of it will make any difference if someone doesn't come beside you, hold your baby on their hip, cook with you. Whatever good I did there, I did it by sitting down with people, entering their lives."

We learn to love because our friends have loved us.

Jesus Himself taught by friendship. One of my friends says, "For God so loved the world that he didn't send a committee."

The heart of Christianity is that instead of sending another ten commandments, God gave Himself in the person of Jesus and through the Holy Spirit.

It's remarkable, really, when you think about it. In God's most shocking act of revelation, He took on human nature, a particular body at a particular time. What a wild and unbelievable thing! Creation must have been shot through with shock when the almighty God entered our temporal realm, when the timeless maker of time limited Himself to the passing away of days. All the angels must have leaned in with curiosity, muttering over their shoulders to one another, "What would the eternal God do as a human? How will He finally teach these fumbling humans to be good? Will He bring down fire from the heavens? Will He do some marvelous, incontestable miracle so that all through the ages, no one, not even Richard Dawkins or Stephen Hawking, could doubt His mighty power? Will He write the principles of His mission in indelible golden letters on an unmovable rock? Will He bring, at last, the opulent and oppressive government of Rome to its knees?"

The reality of Jesus' life is almost underwhelming. He did miracles, yes, and some simple, needy people were won over by the grace of His healing hands. But the miracles were not showy or incontestable; even the religious leaders were not convinced of their veracity. He taught, and as One with authority, but His teaching was not like the heady Greek philosophy of His day or the meticulous legality of the Pharisees. For the most part, His teaching was simple, earthy, and story driven; His parables and similes spoke of the humble and the familiar—houses and farms and women and coins and lost sons.

The majority of Jesus' ministry was preoccupied with the prosaic business of friendship. He did not appear to have picked

His disciples for their excellent character or their exceptional intelligence and learnedness. In fact, most of them were rather unremarkable—disappointing, even. A garden variety of bozos, ready to withhold food from a hungry crowd and curse their ideological opponents and scatter at the sight of an arrest. His followers were women of ill repute and sisters who got into arguments over doing the dishes. Jesus chose to spend most of His earthly time with these people—telling them stories, eating with them, traveling with them, teaching them to pray.

I wonder if Jesus' eyes sparkled with secret surprises just like Gwennie's.

When He knew His time had come, that His death was near, and that these would be the last words He would tell his disciples, His message was simple:

> I have loved you even as the Father has loved me. Remain in my love. When you obey my commandments, you remain in my love, just as I obey my Father's commandments and remain in his love. I have told you these things so that you will be filled with my joy. Yes, your joy will overflow! This is my commandment: Love each other in the same way I have loved you. There is no greater love than to lay down one's life for one's friends. You are my friends if you do what I command. I no longer call you slaves, because a master doesn't confide in his slaves. *Now you are my friends.*
>
> JOHN 15:9-15, EMPHASIS ADDED

The wonderful secret of Christianity is that truth is found not in a principle but in a person. All these years later, what the church has passed down is not a long list of affirmable, cold facts but the life of love and the Spirit of life Himself. And the way life has been passed down is through the commitment and companionship of His earthly, fumbling friends. Those people, men and women, who walked with Him on this earth guarded the memory of His life, the mystery of His death, and the majesty of His resurrection—to the point of their own deaths. What they preserved and passed down to us is life with Jesus, friendship with God, wisdom passed to us through the wounded hands of the Savior. In Communion, we experience the greatest love that Jesus spoke of: a man who laid down His life for His friends.

Any Christian mentorship worth its salt must remember this: Jesus taught through friendship.

Friendship Will Change the World

I am firmly of the belief that all of us are called to invest our lives in something bigger than ourselves. What were we put on this planet for if not to love, teach, care for, heal, protect, create, and change the world to our greatest ability? And those of us who are Christians are called to live our lives for the Kingdom of God. This phrase—"the Kingdom of God"—can seem vague or heavy, carrying with it both too many connotations and not enough. But very simply, it means living a life that wishes for God's will to be done on earth as it is in heaven—in other words, for God's ways of love, kindness, justice, beauty, and forgiveness to be done. It means living so that our neighborhood, city, country, and generation can see and feel God's redemption. And I think the role of friendship in living this way cannot be overemphasized.

Gwennie and my mom have taught me two important things

about living a life committed to ministry, mentorship, and the Kingdom. First, change is passed through relationships. And second, all it takes to be a person who changes the world is the willingness to say yes.

The relatively short years my mom and Gwennie spent together in Eastern Europe marked them and touched my life, too, as I was loved and mentored by both of them. For them, faith was not only knitted into the fabric of life; it made up all the threads. I grew up knowing that God was with us at teatime, in the car as we all belted Andrea Bocelli at the top of our lungs, as we cooked, as we watched the sunset, and as we were moved by the humorous and yet sincere pathos of *Bleak House*. We were Jesus' disciples, and He was with us always. All moments were a testament to His love, His kindness, His faithfulness, and the hope He offered.

Many of the biggest movements of history were started and sustained by friendships. The Romantic movement, whose ripples are still being felt in politics, philosophy, and literature, allegedly got its inauspicious start in the Wordsworth living room, where William and his siblings would discuss poetry and philosophy. Or one could look to the Inklings, perhaps the most influential writing group of the twentieth century, which started as a group of friends who met at a pub to discuss their writing projects.

If I want to change the world and live in a way that speaks of God's grace and mercy, the first step is to do so through friendship, through communion, through love. All the tricks and media and programs in the world cannot make up for that kind of impact.

The second step to changing the world is to live a life where you are willing to say yes.

What was the difference between the disciples and the other fishermen standing around the day Jesus chose His twelve? What was the difference between my mother and Gwennie and all the other people who attended the same conference but chose not to go to Eastern Europe? The difference was that they were willing to say yes, to count the cost, to follow Jesus anywhere, to see themselves as capable of being a part of God's plan for bringing wholeness, justice, peace, and kindness to the world.

Everyone can change the world. Even if it is only your neighborhood, you can have a longer and deeper impact than you can imagine. This will look different for every person. We are each given a different puzzle, different opportunities, different challenges to overcome, different skills, and different arenas, but we can all live with purpose, and we are all called to help others, to pass on the wisdom that has been given to us. I tend to think we all have more capacity than we think we have to do so. You would be surprised what you are capable of if you throw yourself into it.

I think this kind of world-changing requires an identity shift. You must begin to see yourself as someone with something to give, whether that's a meal for your struggling friend, wisdom to pass on (even if it is only to say, "Do not do what I have done"), or resources to use, even if the only resource you possess is love.

Let me assure you: you have something to give.

I saw this most clearly on display when I was a resident adviser. My sophomore year I took on a responsibility I couldn't have even imagined: being the dorm mother to fifty-six girls. I had a partner RA, and we did all we could to make university a place conducive for our residents' intellectual, spiritual, emotional, and social growth. This involved planning events for the girls to connect over, being available for pastoral conversations when people encountered stresses away from home, and enforcing rules to make the dorm a place where everyone could feel safe and cared for. Doing all this while being students ourselves was, at times, absolutely exhausting. But it was also fulfilling; I learned a great deal. In time, I began to notice a pattern: there were three kinds of residents.

The first group were the disengaged residents. These students came to college with their heads down, ready to work, get good grades, and emerge into adulthood with GPAs and recommendations for the adult life they wished to create. I never blamed these residents, and if I'm honest, I may have fallen into this category at times myself—happy to do my own thing and not get caught in the hullabaloo. But I felt that these students were missing out. Our school was uniquely close-knit, and by choosing not to engage, they missed a lot of delight and a lot of opportunities for growth. Watching them made me wonder how much I had missed when I'd simply disengaged too.

The second group I called the extracurricular kids. They saw college as a summer camp and me as their camp counselor, there to make life wonderful for them. These students came to college ready to love it. They were in every club, ready to meet their college BFF, and in awe of every event or gathering they attended. They wanted me to be their mentor, friend, and party planner. I loved their enthusiasm, but as the year wore on, they began to wear on me.

After every event I planned, they would ask, "So, what's next?" leaving me to try to hide exasperation from my exhausted face.

Ask me that in a week or two, once I've had a break, okay? I'd think to myself.

Often they'd come to me with suggestions for parties I could host or new floor traditions I could begin, but they never seemed to harbor the idea that they might be able to help me pull off those things. Unlike the disengaged students, they drank deeply from the communal well, enjoyed life to the fullest, and were satisfied with their experiences. They did not, however, see themselves as having any obligation to give back to the community.

And then there was the third group: the citizens. I use this word because it implies both a give and a take. Citizens should be able to expect something of their country: certain rights and freedoms, roads, protection, and just leadership. But good citizens also give back to the country they've learned to love; they care for their city, they invest in their schools, they vote. This is what the citizen-students were like. They soaked up the activities, resources, and homeliness we provided. But they also actively contributed to the ecosystem of our community. The key characteristic I saw in all of them was thankfulness. Even though I was doing my job, they always received my work with a kind of surprised delight. They were the ones who stayed after events to help me clean up. They left notes of thanks before going home on breaks. And more than anything, they took ownership of the floor. As the year wore on, they took what I gave them and began to exert their own creativity. They came to me with ideas for parties and asked if they could help plan or host them. With them, I felt like my work was worth it—first, because they were thankful for it and second, because they began to make their own imprint on the floor. One of my greatest delights was to watch as those girls who took initiative became RAs themselves the next year.

The citizen-students had the same attitude that my mom and

Gwennie had: *I can do this! I have something to give! I can help! It's my duty, joy, and calling to give back.*

I want to end this book with a simple admonition: you have something to give to the world. Give it!

The wonderful thing about friendship is that it calls us out of ourselves and into someone else's world. We are not meant to be isolated, and friends give us the gifts of love, companionship, and kindness. But those gifts will become stale, self-centered, and small if we do not reach out and give them to someone else. You have something to give, and the world desperately needs it. You do not need a program or a book (though I hope you can use this one!). All you need is to think of yourself as a citizen of this world and of God's Kingdom, someone who receives love and therefore richly gives it.

The Gift of Love

The gift of friendship is really the gift of love. Henri Nouwen, one of my favorite authors, writes that the greatest gift we can give each other is the gift of our belovedness: knowing that deep down, our identity is as someone who is beloved by God and then is called to share that generous love with others.

When I reflect on how well I have been loved by friends and family over the years, tears well up in my eyes. I have done nothing to deserve that love, but that is the nature of love. It gives itself generously; it sees the value and beauty in every person and every story. The beauty of friendship is that as we love someone, we begin a new story, and we become something new. The bond of friendship never leaves us unchanged. It grows our hearts bigger and bigger. Love never runs out; it just expands our capacity to love. So to love others, to be on the lookout for kindred spirits, is to never stop hoping. The gift of belovedness, and of friendship, is one of the greatest ways we can participate in God's nature and love. Let us take that seriously.

So I give you this encouragement and this charge:

You are beloved.

Now go love someone else.

About the Authors

SALLY CLARKSON is the beloved author of multiple bestselling books, including *Own Your Life*, *The Lifegiving Home* (with her daughter Sarah), *Desperate* (with Sarah Mae), and *Different* (with her son Nathan). As a mother of four, she has inspired thousands of women through conferences, resources, and books with Whole Heart Ministries (www.wholeheart.org). She has also advocated relentlessly for the power of motherhood and the influence of home through her Mom Heart conferences (www .momheart.org), speaking to audiences on several continents.

Discipleship and mentoring women to understand how to love God in a more personal way and how to live a satisfying Christian life are threads through all of Sally's messages. She encourages many through her blogs, podcasts, and websites. You can find her on her blog at www.sallyclarkson.com. Her popular podcast, *At Home with Sally Clarkson and Friends*, with over a million downloads, can be found on iTunes and Stitcher. She regularly teaches at conferences and on webcasts, and she participates in international discipleship ministry in venues all over the world.

SARAH CLARKSON is an author, a blogger, and a student of theology. She graduated from Wycliffe Hall in Oxford with a bachelor's degree in theology, where she also spent a proud year as president of the Oxford University C. S. Lewis Society. She's the author of *Read for the Heart* (a guide to children's literature), *Caught Up in a Story* (on the formative power of story), *Journeys of Faithfulness* (a creative, contemplative devotional for young women), and *Book Girl* (a journey through the treasures of a reading life). Through blogs, books, and her current research, she explores the theological significance of story, the intersection of theology and imagination, and the formative power of beauty. She writes regularly about her adventures at sarahclarkson.com and is at slow work on a novel. She can often be found with a cup of good coffee in one of the many quaint corners amid Oxford's "dreaming spires," where she lives in a red-doored cottage with her husband, Thomas, and their daughter, Lilian.

JOY CLARKSON is a lover of God and people, a crafter of words, and a dedicated evangelist for the soul-enriching benefits of teatime. She studied rhetorical communications at Biola University, where she competed on the speech and debate team as a champion of parliamentary debate. She is currently working on her doctorate in theology, imagination, and the arts at the University of St. Andrews in Scotland, where she enjoys long walks on the shore of the North Sea and visits to tiny fishing villages. She fills her days with academic research, music making, adventuring, and savoring deep conversations with her soul friends. In her spare time, Joy bakes, sings, reads, writes, dabbles in marketing, adores golden retrievers, and drinks too much tea.

Notes

INTRODUCTION

1. Ceylan Yeginsu, "U.K. Appoints a Minister for Loneliness," *New York Times*, January 17, 2018, https://www.nytimes.com/2018/01/17/world/europe/uk -britain-loneliness.html.

CHAPTER 2: THE VOICE OF LONELINESS AND THE VOICE OF LOVE

1. Emily Dickinson, "The Loneliness One Dare Not Sound," http://www .edickinson.org/editions/1/image_sets/236146.
2. This is the title of one of Berry's novels, published in 1967.
3. Marilynne Robinson, *Lila* (London: Virago, 2014), 70.
4. Ibid., 110.
5. Ibid., 34.
6. Ibid., 142.
7. Ibid., 135.
8. Ibid., 253.
9. Ibid., 260.

CHAPTER 5: SATURDAY MORNINGS: THE GIRLS' CLUB PROTOTYPE

1. Wendell Berry, *The Art of the Commonplace: The Agrarian Essays of Wendell Berry*, ed. Norman Wirzba (Berkeley, CA: Counterpoint, 2003), 117–18.
2. *Celtic Daily Prayer: Prayers and Readings from the Northumbria Community* (San Francisco: HarperCollins, 2002), 18–19.

CHAPTER 6: DATING YOUR FRIENDS

1. Joel D. Block and Diane Greenberg, *Women and Friendship* (New York: F. Watts, 1985).
2. C. S. Lewis, *The Four Loves* (New York: Harcourt, 1960), 98.

CHAPTER 8: LOOKING FOR AVONLEA
1. Wendell Berry, *Remembering* (Berkeley, CA: Counterpoint, 2008), 77.
2. Ibid., 48.
3. Elizabeth Goudge, *Pilgrim's Inn* (New York: Coward-McCann, 1948), 48.
4. Ibid.

CHAPTER 11: BECOMING A QUEEN
1. J. R. R. Tolkien, *The Lord of the Rings: Deluxe Illustrated Edition* (New York: Houghton Mifflin, 1991), 957.
2. George Eliot, *Middlemarch* (Hertfordshire, England: Wordsworth Editions, 1994), 688.

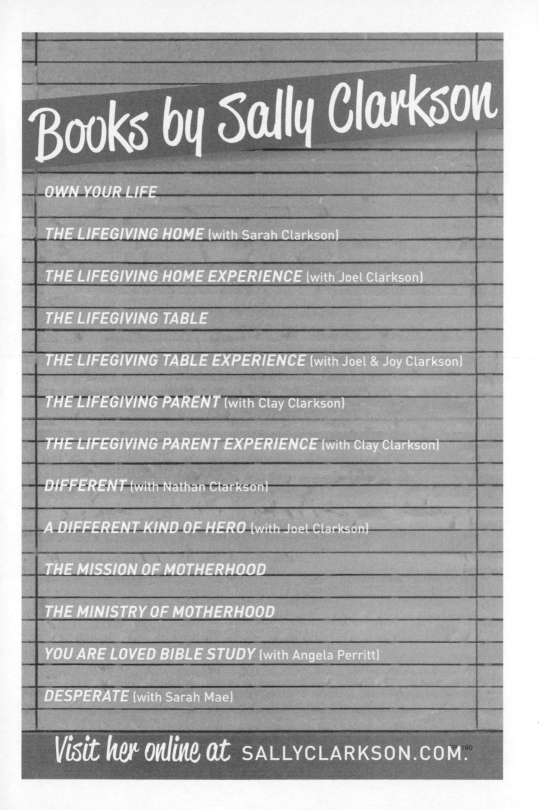

Books by Sally Clarkson

OWN YOUR LIFE

THE LIFEGIVING HOME (with Sarah Clarkson)

THE LIFEGIVING HOME EXPERIENCE (with Joel Clarkson)

THE LIFEGIVING TABLE

THE LIFEGIVING TABLE EXPERIENCE (with Joel & Joy Clarkson)

THE LIFEGIVING PARENT (with Clay Clarkson)

THE LIFEGIVING PARENT EXPERIENCE (with Clay Clarkson)

DIFFERENT (with Nathan Clarkson)

A DIFFERENT KIND OF HERO (with Joel Clarkson)

THE MISSION OF MOTHERHOOD

THE MINISTRY OF MOTHERHOOD

YOU ARE LOVED BIBLE STUDY (with Angela Perritt)

DESPERATE (with Sarah Mae)

Visit her online at SALLYCLARKSON.COM.

Join Sarah Clarkson on your journey to becoming a book girl!

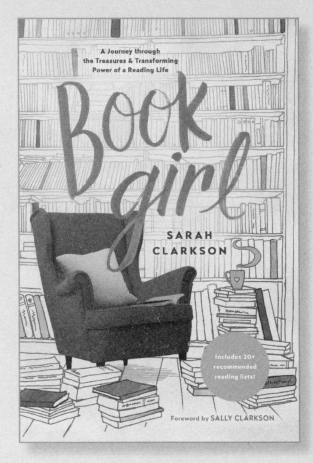

Whether you've long considered yourself a reader or have dreams of becoming one, *Book Girl* will draw you into the lifegiving journey of becoming a woman who reads and lives well.